You Said a Mouthful

Written by
Florence Markoff

Illustrated by
Sandra Feit and Nora L'Heureux

bookmark
productions

Bookmark Productions
Providence, Rhode Island

ISBN: 978-06925960-9-8

The information presented herein represents the views of the author as of the date of the publication. While every attempt has been made to verify the information in this book, the author does not assume any responsibility for errors, inaccuracies, or omissions.

Edited by Stephanie Mann

Printed in the United States of America

Dedication

I dedicate *You Said a Mouthful* to my late husband, Henry W., and my three sons, Joseph, Ronald, and Gary. I appreciated the interest and devotion they have shown me in the writing of this book. Without them, this book would not have been possible.

A portion of the proceeds from the sale of this book will be donated to The Rachel Molly Markoff Foundation, commonly known as Art in Giving. This public charity combines the ingenuity of childhood cancer researchers with the creativity of artists. Researchers stretch the limits of their minds in a relentless pursuit to cure cancer. Artists stretch the limits of their imagination to appeal to our hearts and souls. Art in Giving follows a unique path that combines the creativity and generosity of its artists with the needs of talented cancer researchers. Up to fifty percent of the proceeds from the sale of art through the efforts of Art in Giving are donated to The Rachel Molly Markoff Foundation, a 501(c)(3) public charity that makes research grants to cancer researchers.

To learn more go to www.artingiving.com.

CHAPTER LIST

//

Uncover the history and
mystery of how our language
became garnished with
words related to food.

//

H ave you ever been given the cold shoulder? Or been sold a lemon? Were you ever curious how Graham crackers got their name? Or Salisbury steak? Harvard beets? Have you ever wondered who Little Jack Horner was? And what about his famous plum?

You Said a Mouthful is a fascinating collection of stories behind the food expressions we hear and say every day. From doggie bags to sugar cubes, from Baked Alaska to pie in the sky, *You Said a Mouthful* uncovers the history and mystery of how our language became garnished with words related to food. *You Said a Mouthful* has universal appeal because everyone knows expressions like:

But more than that, everyone eats! Young and old alike will be amused and intrigued to learn the origin of peanut butter, pretzels, and Melba toast. They will also find it fascinating to discover the connections between commonly used phrases and well-known historical figures like Napoleon, Thomas Jefferson, and William Shakespeare.

For a long time, this book has been simmering on the back burner of my mind. It is an extension of a radio feature I have been doing for many years: "There's a Word for It" tells the stories behind words we hear and say every day.

In my etymological wanderings, I noticed that the names of foods have fascinating stories, and I began to trace how they entered our everyday language. *You Said a Mouthful* aims to give an entertaining and informative sampling of the thousands of words and phrases that relate to the foods we eat.

You Said a Mouthful makes no pretension to authority, nor does it lay claim to linguistic scholarship. It makes no effort to prove or disprove theories that have been advanced regarding the origin and development of certain words we speak. Rather, it is an attempt to share the fascination I feel for words. I am deeply indebted to the many word lovers and scholars listed in the bibliography for their groundbreaking and painstaking research. Certainly I have sinned by omission, but this is a selection of just what one person considered to be the most interesting food words of their kind.

I sincerely hope that you get as much pleasure from reading this book as I did from writing it, and that you will be left with a deeper appreciation of the words we "eat."

Bon appétit!

Florence Markoff
Providence, Rhode Island
December 2015

You Said a Mouthful

//

The pretzel was discovered back in the sixteenth century by a German monk who was a schoolteacher. The monk promised his students a special reward for learning their prayers.

//

There you are at the cocktail party, wearing a cocktail dress, sipping a cocktail made in a cocktail shaker, listening to a cocktail pianist playing background music.

The cocktail party has become an American institution and the word *cocktail* has interesting stories. One story takes us back to Dobbs Ferry, New York, when General George Washington's officers were stationed there in 1777. Barmaid Betsy Flanagan served the men a special drink made from rum, rye, and fruit juices. She decorated the glass with tail feathers from a neighbor's rooster. An inspired French soldier in the group made a toast. "*Vive le coq's* tail!" he said. And that is how, according to one story, the legend of the cocktail was born.

Another story of the cocktail describes a warm afternoon in New Orleans in the mid-1800s. A customer walked into the drugstore of Mr. Antoine Peychaud. The customer felt sick. Mr. Peychaud prescribed a shot of brandy with bitters. Since he had nothing to serve it in, he found an egg in which he usually mixed his prescriptions called a *coquetier* (pronounced kok-tee-yay). The man felt better after drinking it, and told all his friends about the great-tasting drink that cured him so fast. It wasn't long before *coquetier* became the famous *cocktail*.

Let's move over to the cocktail table to see what's offered.
The cheese and crackers look appetizing. What a choice of cheese! Oh, by the way, did I mention that most cheeses are named for the locations

they come from? Camembert comes from the village of Camembert in Normandy; Cheddar was first made in the Somerset village of Cheddar; Brie comes from France in the Brie district of Seine-et-Marne; Edam and Gouda both come from Holland near Amsterdam; Parmesan is from Parma in northern Italy and Roquefort from Roquefort in southwest France; and Gorgonzola, the cheese with the strong smell, comes from the Italian village of Gorgonzola near Milan.

The word *cheese* is sometimes used in a pejorative way to mean "it smells." In the late eighteenth century, the term *cheesy* meant *worthless* or *bad.*

The best-known US cheese is simply called American cheese. It was so called after the Revolutionary War, when proud American dairy workers looked down on anything that came from England. American cheese became more popular when a Chicago grocery clerk named J. H. Kraft had the idea of wrapping individual portions of cheese for his customers. In 1903, he traveled by horse and wagon and sold his cheese from door to door.

How about a cracker for your cheese?

The cracker is a crisp, hard flour wafer that gets its name from the cracking sound it makes when broken. It's also the source of many delectable sayings: Things aren't always what they're cracked up to be and it's not always easy to crack a smile or crack a joke when you have a hard nut to crack. Sometimes you have to crack down on the crackpot who can crack up if you don't crack the whip. Maybe it's time to crack the books.

May I offer you an hors d'oeuvre?

The French gave us hors d'oeuvres and we've been forever grateful. In the United States, *hors d'oeuvre* means "outside of the meal." Hors d'oeuvres are little varied appetizers, hot or cold, usually served with cocktails before the meal.

The phrase is often butchered in pronunciation, from the singular *horse doover* to the plural *horse doovers*. Please taste the correct *oar derv* or *oar dervs*.

How about sampling the canapés?

Canapé (pronounced kan-uh-pay) took a long, roundabout way to become a piece of bread or toast topped with savory food. The word can be traced back to the term *canopy*, which is a piece of fabric draped on posts over a bed and used as a decorative touch. This derives from the Greek word *konopeion*, which was a mosquito netting used to cover people up, protecting them from being bitten by mosquitoes. This idea of "covering up" was used by the French to describe an hors d'oeuvre consisting of a piece of toast covered up with a tasty topping.

What's a cocktail party without potato chips?

Potato chips started their munchy career in the summer of 1853 at an elegant resort in Saratoga, New York. George Crum was employed as a chef at Moon Lake Lodge, where the restaurant menu featured the standard thick-cut French fried potatoes brought to the United States by Thomas Jefferson from France when he was ambassador to that country. One evening at Moon Lake Lodge, a dinner guest found Chef Crum's French fries too thick for his liking and sent back the order to the kitchen. Crum cut and fried a thinner batch, but these, too, met with disapproval. Frustrated, Crum decided to produce French fries so thin you couldn't pick them up with a fork. Much to Crum's great surprise, the guest was ecstatic over the browned, paper-thin potatoes, and other guests began to ask for Crum's potato chips. They began to appear on the menu as Saratoga chips, a house specialty.

And don't forget the pretzel. Bite into a crunchy morsel as I tell you about this cracker's interesting history.

The pretzel was discovered back in the sixteenth century by a German monk who was a schoolteacher. The monk promised his students a special reward for learning their prayers. He took thin strips of dough and twisted them into a knot. The shape of the pastry suggested the folded arms of a person at prayer. The monks didn't know what to call the new food, so they decided on an old Latin word, *pretiola*, which means *little reward*. In England, *pretiola* was changed to pretzel—and pretzel it has remained since.

//

Borscht became so famous that in

the 1930s people began referring to

resorts in the Catskill Mountains

featuring Jewish entertainers

as the "Borscht Belt."

//

I f you enjoy a bowl of hot soup on a cold winter's day, you're talking about a liquid food made of boiled ingredients with an infinite number of variations.

Let's start off with consommé, a clear soup every good cook says it takes an unconscionable amount of time to cook. In French, the word *consommer* means *to finish* and the broth is so named because it requires endless boiling of meat for the finished product.

Travel the world and you'll discover soup's popularity.

The Italians have a patriotic loyalty to their national soup called *minestra*, simply meaning *soup*. Americans know it as *minestrone*, which translates to *big soup*.

France gave us two famous soups. The first, *julienne*, was made famous by Julien, the French caterer whose landmark was cutting the vegetables for his soup in narrow strips. Julien lived in Boston at the time of the French Revolution. His restaurant was on Milk Street, where French refugees escaping from the Reign of Terror in France would order *soupe julienne*.

The second famous French soup is a delectable cold soup considered one of the top delicacies of French cuisine. It was created by Louis Diat, a chef in the New York Ritz-Carlton Hotel in 1917. He called the soup *vichyssoise* because he had grown up in the city of Vichy. During World War II, many French chefs tried to change the name of the soup because of their hatred for the wartime government established by the Nazis in the city of Vichy.

India makes its own special soup contribution with the fascinating *mulligatawny*. This soup was created while India was still part of the British Commonwealth. *Mulligatawny* is an Anglicized version of the words *milagu tannir*, meaning *pepper water*.

The Russians and Poles introduced the famous beet and cabbage soup known as borscht. Borscht became so famous that in the 1930s people began referring to resorts in the Catskill Mountains featuring Jewish entertainers as the "Borscht Belt."

Soup sometimes left the table and moved into the language in a soupy way.

People who had difficulties were in the soup when they found themselves in a pea-soup fog, and they drove cars that were souped up. The phrase "souped up" was most commonly used in connection with an automobile installed with superchargers as if giving the engine an explosive new power.

Still there is something glamorous about soup. When men get all dressed up in white tie and tails for a formal dinner, they are described as "wearing their soup and fish." This formal attire used to be worn at dinners where the first two courses were soup and fish, and the meal was complete "from soup to nuts."

//

The words "fish or cut bait" appeared in

the halls of Congress back in 1876, when

Joseph Gurney Cannon, a representative

from Illinois, said the phrase on the

floor of the House of Congress

for the first time.

//

I f you think this is going to be a fishy story, you're right—it is!

Now let's understand one another. I'm not fishing for compliments when I invite you to join me on a fishing expedition. Let's just test the waters and talk about how fish is not only part of our everyday diet, but is also included in our everyday conversation.

We all know the outstanding characteristic of the fish is its habitat, and that almost all fish breathe by means of gills. It's the fish's breathing that causes it to be open-mouthed and look as if it were drinking all the time. This constant swallowing must have inspired the habit of describing a person who is loaded to the gills as one who drinks like a fish.

Now if a fish smells, its freshness is questionable. And so the word *fishy* came to mean *doubtful*. Hence, the phrase *fishy story* comes from the fact that fishermen, especially those who fish for sport rather than their livelihood, are famous for proudly exaggerating the size of their catch. Through the years, *fishy story* came to mean *tall tale*.

The poet Eugene Field wrote, "It is always the biggest fish you catch that gets away." Even if the biggest fish does get away, we take comfort in knowing there are lots of other fish in the sea—and plenty of other fish to fry.

At this point in our story, I think you'll agree that fish swam into our language and did very well for fish out of water.

Sometimes you might act like a cold fish when you speak firmly to someone, saying, "Fish or cut bait!" This phrase is often used when referring to politicians who won't take a position on an issue.

In fact, the words "fish or cut bait" appeared in the halls of Congress back in 1876, when Joseph Gurney Cannon, a representative from Illinois, said the phrase on the floor of the House of Congress for the first time. The congressional record printed his remarks that read, "Now I want you gentlemen in the House to fish or cut bait. Do something positive for once during this session." Just how this expression moved from fish to politics is a question we'll have to swim with, I'm afraid.

We do know, however, that cutting bait is one of the essential duties on board a deep-sea fishing vessel. Live fish, carried for that purpose, are cut into chunks which are then dropped overboard to attract the quarry when the boat has reached a favorable location.

The earliest record of the phrase "neither fish nor fowl" coincided in time with the disagreement between King Henry VIII of England and Pope Clement VII during the sixteenth century. At the time, depending on whether people continued to eat fish or fowl on days of fasting, they were declared to be either religious or irreligious. We picked up the expression in the United States, where anything that can't be definitely classified is referred to as neither fish nor fowl.

There are times when we find ourselves in a pretty kettle of fish, and discover we're in deep trouble. The expression developed from a custom of the people who lived along the River Tweed in London. It was usual at the time (1785) for gentlemen who lived near the river to entertain their friends with a celebration they called "a kettle of fish."

There were times when things went awry. The chowder burned, the salt was forgotten, or the kettle overturned. In any such instance, the party would be ruined and it turned out to be a pretty kettle of fish.

I notice that at this point you're giving me the fish eye. This tells me that I've been a fish out of water for long enough. And if I'm not careful, I'll start to sound like a fishwife who acts like a big fish in a small pond.

Holy mackerel! I almost forgot one more item about a special fish that couldn't possibly live in a fish bowl. The source is anonymous for this, but the story tells us about the hiccup, a type of fish from Brazil. Hiccups can grow to reach a length of twelve feet. They can swallow so much water, and then expel it with such force, that the sound can be heard miles away. (This might be a red herring, but I think I just heard a sound that exploded like a hiccup.)

I wonder: Is it possible that the story of the hiccup is just another fishy story? Well, yes—it's possible!

You Said a Mouthful

II

The word *goose* comes from the Old English word *gos*. Since the sixteenth century, the term has been applied to a foolish or silly person because the bird was considered to be stupid.

II

The goose was found to be plentiful in the New World, but it has never been as successfully marketed as the chicken or the turkey. What the goose lacked, however, in culinary fame, it made up for in its contribution to the English language.

The word *goose* comes from the Old English word *gos*. Since the sixteenth century, the term has been applied to a foolish or silly person because the bird was considered to be stupid. Today, we still hear a foolish person called "a silly goose."

The male goose is a gander. One of the timeworn English sayings we still use today is "what's sauce for the goose is sauce for the gander." It appeared in John Ray's 1670 collection of proverbs, and in essence means "equality for all."

Mother Goose became synonymous with nursery rhymes about 1760 when a collection entitled *Mother Goose's Melody* was published in London. Mother Goose, however, had nothing to do with her namesake. "Goose" was simply a shortened form of her real name, which was Elizabeth Vergoose.

"The goose that laid the golden egg" comes to us from Aesop's Fables. The farmer who owned the goose wanted to get the mass of gold he thought must be inside her, so he cut her open, and she died. Aesop's moral is now enshrined in the proverb "don't kill the goose that laid the golden egg."

Goosestep referred to a military exercise in England in 1806. It required recruits to stand on one leg while swinging the other back and forth. This form of calisthenics, which was used in most European armies, was called *goosestep* because it resembled the stiff-legged walk of a goose.

By the end of the nineteenth century, the term referred to a slow, straight-legged marching step. In the early 1930s, it became associated with the Nazi marching step. Mussolini joined Hitler in the goosestep march, and ever since, it has been connected with Fascism and dictatorship.

Goose egg for *zero* is an American term that goes back to the 1850s. (The British say *duck egg*.) From 1866 on, it became common baseball language, and it is also related to the term for zero in tennis, *love*, which comes from the French word for egg, *l'oeuf*.

In the early 1890s, the phrase "to goose someone" took on its vulgar present-day meaning of poking someone between the buttocks in order to startle him or her. The origin of this phrase isn't generally known, but one theory is that it made the victim cry out like a goose. Another explanation comes from the fact that the goose is a pugnacious bird that sometimes attacks human beings by snapping at them. Because of the goose's height, the buttocks is the part of the human body it can reach most easily.

Another possibility has to do with the farmer's custom of examining a goose before it is let out to feed in a field. He feels its bottom for an egg about to be laid. If an egg is there, the goose is kept penned up until it lays.

You Said a Mouthful

//

For many years, a small pig-shaped
bank for holding coins has been called
a *piggy bank*. The word came from the
Old English word *pygg*, meaning an
earthenware pitcher or jar.

//

Meat is an example of a word that isn't what it used to be. It has changed its meaning through the years, and its meaning has become narrower in its development. In Old English, the word meant food of any kind, but more particularly solid food in contrast to liquids. This is pointed out in combinations of words such as *sweetmeat* (a piece of candy) and *nutmeat* (the edible part of a nut). In later times, *meat* came to mean *animal flesh* in contrast to fish and poultry.

In the late 1920s, Americans used the word *meathooks* for *hands* and *meatball* for *a dull, boring person*. Mincemeat is a mixture of currants, raisins, sugar, apples, candied peel, spices, and often suet. It sounds delicious, but when you "make mincemeat of someone," that person is utterly defeated.

Beef is the meat of a full-grown steer, ox, cow, or bull. The French started off by calling it *boeuf*, and we took it over as *beef*. Americans had developed a great appetite for beef by the turn of the nineteenth century. In the 1880s, steakhouses were among the most popular restaurants in large American cities. The word *beef* has also joined the language of American slang. When you beef, you complain, and when something is beefed up, it is made more vigorous.

Let's face it: Pigs have never had good public relations, and phrases connected with the pig are usually negative.

While some biologists say pigs are quite intelligent, a person who is called a *pig* is accused of filth, greed, gluttony, and obesity. To pig out or be piggish is to overeat, and a pig pen or pigsty refers to a room or house that is a miserable, filthy place.

In Great Britain, *pig* was slang for a policeman, a usage picked up by anti-establishment groups in the United States during the 1960s. Furthermore, pigs are commonly thought to be as obstinate as mules and, for centuries, *pigheaded* has meant *stubborn*.

Considering the background of the pig, it hardly seems likely that anyone would wish to ride a pig; indeed, the term *piggyback* doesn't refer to the animal. Rather, it is a corruption of *pick-a-back*, meaning to carry something or someone on one's back or shoulders.

The phrase "a pig in a poke" reminds us to take a close look at our purchase before parting with our money. In old-time markets, frauds were frequently carried out when a young pig was put on display, and the seller was supposed to be offering others tied in sacks, or pokes, ready to carry away. When those who bought them got home, they found not a pig, but a cat. Any sharp buyer would insist on opening the bag in the market before buying. If the trader had been dishonest, the buyer would let the cat out of the bag.

For many years, a small pig-shaped bank for holding coins has been called a *piggy bank*. The word came from the Old English word *pygg*, meaning an earthenware pitcher or jar. Years later, pig-shaped pottery coin containers for children became popular.

The pig is remembered even after it is gone. The hide called *pigskin* makes very good leather used for gloves, handbags, luggage, and other products. It is also used to cover American footballs, and since the late 1990s, the football itself has been called a *pigskin*. On occasion, the male chauvinist pig has been in the spotlight, while one who over-indulges is said to make a pig of himself. And if you don't agree with his opinions, he might even say, "In a pig's eye!"

It's safe to say that, when it comes to food, the pig manages to keep in the culinary frontline.

Bacon is the cured meat from the back and sides of a pig. In Germany, bacon was a favorite food for centuries. Wild pigs, or *bachen*, roamed the forests, and some believe *bachen* was the beginning of *bacon*. The famous expression "to bring home the bacon" means to have general success in an undertaking, as well as simply bringing home the pay-check.

Would you believe the lowly pig managed to get into government circles? *Pork barrel* describes government funds for highways, bridges, or other local improvements that are intended to ingratiate congressmen with their constituents. The phrase originated on Southern plantations in the pre-Civil War period when slaves were given salt pork from huge barrels. Sometimes the eagerness of the slaves would make them try to take as much as they could for themselves. Members of Congress, in the rush to get their local appropriations approved, behaved much like the hungry slaves. Their bills were facetiously called *pork barrel bills.*

Our society has certainly given the pig much attention. We even speak Pig Latin, which is a sort of mock Latin as pigs might speak it. Each word begins with its first vowel, so *Pig Latin* would be *Igpay Atinlay*.

But one of the most outstanding testimonials to the pig is a hairstyle that has been worn for generations. It's a tight, narrow braid of hair hanging down the back of the head and is said to resemble the animal's tail. Hence the name *pigtail*.

The pig's close relative is the hog. In England, a shilling was once called a *hog*, while in the United States, a ten-cent piece was given the same nickname. To spend the whole hog at one time would have been to go hog-wild with money.

You may think this is all hogwash, which is the kitchen garbage given to hogs. And so any worthless or meaningless issue has come to be called *hogwash*. Since the most tender and expensive cuts of meat from a hog are high on the animal's body, to eat the high part is to eat well.

Therefore, to live a high lifestyle, especially one with plenty of money and material goods, is to live high on the hog. I would caution you, however, not to be a road-hog and hog the road when you drive.

Ham is the dried thigh of the hog's hind leg. It can be smoked or cured; either way, it plays an important role, not only in the American diet, but in the language as well. The word comes from an Old English term, *hamme*, meaning *the bend of the knee*.

Ham plays a starring role in the theater as a ham actor who is known as a loud, boisterous performer. In Shakespeare's *Hamlet*, players are warned not to "strut and bellow," which is what the ham actor does when he gives a hammy performance. *Ham actor* may also come from the fact that actors once used ham fat to remove their makeup, or it may come from the Cockney English accent that twists the word *amateur* into *hamateur*.

Then again, there was Hamish McCullough, an actor during the mid-1800s. He used to make regular tours of Midwestern states with his own troupe of players. Audiences nicknamed them *Ham's Actors*.

Have you ever wondered why we ask for a rasher of bacon?
Some have suggested that it is so called because, being thin, it may be cooked rashly, or quickly. Others prefer to believe that the word comes from the long-obsolete verb *to rash*, meaning *to cut or slash*. Another theory suggests that *rasher* is a misspelling of *rasure*, a thin slice. This word comes from the Latin verb *redere*, meaning *to scrape, shave, or scratch*.

The Italians came up with a veal and ham dish that was as attractive as it was delicious. One poetic gastronome thought it looked so appetizing that he exclaimed, "*Saltimbocca!*" which means *it leaps into the mouth*.

Are you beginning to think this is all bologna? Also spelled *baloney* and *balony*, this smoked, seasoned sausage is made from a variety of meats, and is popular as a sandwich filling. Bologna comes from the Italian city of Bologna, where it was first produced. The man who made the word famous in everyday conversation was Al Smith, governor of New York and presidential candidate in 1928. His celebrated remark was, "No matter how you slice it, it's still baloney." And when you don't quite believe a comment, you may reply, "Oh, that's a lot of baloney."

So you were ignored and given the cold shoulder. This expression goes back two hundred years and comes from English eating habits.

In those days, people ate very little bread, fruit, or vegetables. Beef, pork, and mutton were all served at a single meal. Anything left over was given to the servants, and a roast was prepared for the following meal. When guests overstayed their welcome, the host had a way of giving a subtle hint: Cold, unpalatable meat was served. After eating "cold shoulder" for a few meals, the guest got the message and eventually left.

What could symbolize American food better than hot dogs and hamburgers?

Served in buns, they are inexpensive, fast to cook, and easy to eat, even while you're standing. When the hot dog is eaten without a roll but accompanied by beans, the dish is called *franks and beans*. Little frankfurters wrapped in puff pastry are called *pigs in a blanket* and are usually served at cocktail parties.

Hot dogs became such a popular food that "hot dog!" became an exclamation of approval. The more emphatic "hot diggety dog!" was later shortened to simply "hot diggety!"

It's possible that the hot dog has grown tame since it's been overcome by the hamburger in popularity. But I ask you, is there anything more delicious than a good, old-fashioned, juicy hot dog with mustard and relish on a toasted bun? It's enough to make you say "hot diggety dog!"

There has been much controversy about the expressions "rule the roost" and "rule the roast." So which is it?

"To rule the roost" refers to the cock who rules the chicken coop. "To rule the roast" refers to the lord of the manor; as master of the house, it was he who presided over the carving of roast meat at the table.

The truth may never be known because early explanations are found for both versions. What complicates things further is that *roost* was formerly pronounced *roast*. In any case, the expression means the same. Whether you rule the roost or rule the roast, you're mighty powerful. In fact, you may even be "roasted" at a formal or informal gathering. At such an event, you would be made the butt of good-natured ridicule. But watch out! This butt, or guest of honor, is sometimes left with the bill, having to pay for his own roast.

Here's a mish-mash of a concoction, with a story as interesting as its name.

Marie de Médicis, wife of Henry IV of France, had an appetite for unusual foods. One of her favorite snacks was a combination of veal, chicken, and turkey combined with pickled herring, onions, and boiled eggs. The entire mixture was all chopped together and served with oil. It was given the name *salmagundi* because it was a combination of the first and last names of her ladies-in-waiting. Washington Irving used the name of the dish for a magazine he edited in the 1800s, and it was also adopted by a club of prominent New York writers and artists. *Salmagundi* came to mean a mishmash of a variety of things brought together in one place.

A similar but less appetizing stew is *gallimaufry*. Though familiar to almost everyone, this French word's origin is uncertain. The French are well-known for their creative culinary masterpieces, even from leftover food. But here in the United States, *gallimaufry* is a stew of leftovers that is not considered very palatable.

//

The mushroom is a perfect example of
what happens when an Englishman tries
to pronounce a foreign word.

//

The famous vegetables we eat every day get their name from the fact that they are full of life. They grow. But unlike other things that are full of life, vegetables don't move. They sit on the ground and grow quietly.

And because a vegetable is so still, it gave us the word *vegetate*, which means the opposite of *full of life*. Both *vegetable* and *vegetate* come from the Latin *vegetare*, which means *to enliven*.

Isn't it strange that from the same beginning, we get words which mean *full of life* and *not full of life*? This is one of the fascinating quirks of our language.

Many vegetables come from the soil and were named for particular qualities.

Lettuce came from *lactuca*, a milk-giving plant; cabbage is from the French *caboche*, or *head*; broccoli is an import from Italy and took its name from *broccolo*, or *little spike*; *tour*, a French word for *round*, helped name the round root we know as turnip; Brussels sprouts were named for the capitol of Belgium where the plant was developed; and pumpkin came through from a Greek ancestor that meant *cooked by the sun*.

Many vegetables come to us with interesting stories. Take, for example, asparagus, a tasty plant originally known as *sparrow grass*. Its real name, however, came from the Greek *asparagos* and made its first appearance in American cookbooks during the late nineteenth century. The most flavorful asparagus is thin and tender, and should be cooked in as little water as possible. Even the Romans knew this. The Emperor Augustus was quoted as saying, "Quicker than you can cook asparagus!" for anything he wanted done quickly.

We all remember our mothers (and their mothers before them!) saying, "If you want bright eyes and good skin, eat your carrots." People have been planting and growing carrots for centuries.

James Cook, the famous explorer, believed in the importance of carrots in the diet. Back in 1772, when he embarked on his famous voyage to the South Pacific, Cook brought a bin full of carrots on his ship, *The Endeavor*.

People didn't know much about vitamin C in those days, but they did know that the carrot was a very healthy vegetable. Modern medicine has cashed in on the old folklore and produced carotene supplements, which are given today to build up resistance to colds.

The mushroom is a perfect example of what happens when an Englishman tries to pronounce a foreign word.
You'll agree there is nothing "mushy" about mushrooms. When the English saw the umbrella-shaped fungus, they mispronounced the French *mousseron*, which means *meadow mushroom*. *Mushroom* also became a verb meaning *to spread fast*. In this sense, it was first applied to bullets, then to fires, and then to anything that grows rapidly.

In ancient Angola, okra was considered extremely valuable. Tribes made "sharp knife" raids into neighbors' fields to steal the crop, and killed anyone who stood in their way. The Arabs, using the vegetable as a rare delicacy fit for weddings and other special occasions, gave it the name *uehka*, meaning *gift*. In time, *uehka* became *okra*.

The onion is a pungent vegetable that is grown around the world. It is eaten in a wide variety of ways, and is a basic seasoning ingredient for thousands of dishes. The word *onion* is from the Latin *unio*, a oneness or union referring to the many united layers of the onion.

In the American market, onion varieties include the Italian onion, the Spanish onion, the Bermuda onion, and the pearl onion, which got its name from the Romans who used the same name for the pearl used in jewelry.

The onion brought its aroma to the language, where it was used to describe a stupid or boring person. In World War II, the military called a badly executed venture an *onion*, and the prize-fighting world talks about a loser as an *onionhead*. It gained respectability somewhere along the line, because someone who is savvy is said to know his onions.

Talk about strange names for things! There is nothing snippy about the parsnip. The name seems to have no connection to anything, except perhaps to the shape of the plant's root. The plant's original name, *pastinum*, is Latin for *a digging fork*.

The potato is considered one of the most important vegetables in the world. Its name started as a *betata* for sweet potatoes, which the Spanish found in the West Indies in 1526 and introduced to Europe. *Betata* became *patata*, and when it appeared in England, it was called *potato*.

After the discovery of the sweet potato, the Spanish found the white potato, an unrelated plant. Mistaking it for just another variety of sweet potato, they gave it the same name.

The French called the white potato *pomme de terre*, meaning *apple of the earth*. I should warn you that a hot potato is anything too hot to handle, and small potatoes is a label for anything insignificant. *Potato* is used to refer to a person's head, while *potato trap* is used to describe the mouth. And when you call a potato a spud, you refer to the spade-like tool used to dig it out of the ground.

//

When someone reveals a secret,
he spills the beans. The beans in
question go back to the
ancient Greeks' method of
voting on new candidates
for their exclusive clubs.

//

Beans have been eaten and enjoyed throughout the world for thousands of years. Most common in the United States are field beans, which include peas, navy beans, black beans, and kidney beans, along with lima, string, soy, butter, wax, and many other varieties.

The name comes from the Old English word *bean*, and is commonly used in modern, everyday conversation. When someone reveals a secret, he spills the beans. The beans in question go back to the ancient Greeks' method of voting on new candidates for their exclusive clubs. Each member had two beans, one white and one brown, and he could put either one into the jar. The white bean was a "yes" vote, and the brown bean was a "no."

The beans were counted in strict secrecy so that a prospective member would never know how many people had voted against him. Obviously, a high percentage of brown beans would be a real embarrassment. Occasionally, however, a clumsy member would accidentally knock over the jar, and the secret was out. He had spilled the beans.

"Not to know beans" was originally a Boston expression. It referred to the fact that anyone who didn't know how to make beans in Boston, the home of the bean and the cod, would have to be incredibly ignorant.

And when something isn't worth a hill of beans, it has little or no value. The word *hill* was inserted into the phrase to exaggerate the point.

Historians report that Napoleon would not eat string beans because he was afraid he would choke on the strings. But today, most varieties are stringless and are often called *green beans.*

In the kitchen, string beans are still used as vegetables, and in the language they describe a tall, thin person. He might also be called a beanpole, another American way of talking about a lanky person. *Beanpole* takes its name from the tall poles that support climbing bean plants. These are the same plants made famous by Jack and his celebrated beanstalk.

The British, besides addressing a peer as an old bean, use the expression "he knows how many beans make five," meaning "he's no fool." Perhaps that's why, when you use your head, you use your bean—and if you were an accountant, you might be called a bean counter.

Wearing a beanie, or a small cap, indicated that you were a good student who won the local spelling bee back in one-room schoolhouse days. This is the same beanie later worn by first-year college students. And when you're full of beans, you're full of energy.

The well-known Boston baked beans is a recipe originally brought from Africa by New England sea captains.
This dish became closely associated with the city of Boston because of the Puritan women who baked beans on Saturdays. They served

the beans that night for dinner and again on Sundays, since no other cooking was allowed until the Sabbath ended Sunday evening. Because of the association between Bostonians and beans, the city came to be called "Bean Town."

The pea is a climbing plant with edible seeds that are enclosed in long pods. The word *pea* is from the Greek *pison*, which became *pease* in plural. The most widely used variety is the garden pea, and split peas are those which have been dried so that the seeds split in two.

The pea joined the bean in popularity and became a food fashion in seventeenth-century France. Madam de Maintenon, Louis XIV's mistress, called it "a passion and madness." At that time, it was proper to lick green peas from their shells. Perhaps eating peas off a knife shouldn't be considered bad table manners after all!

While a pea-head with a pea-brain is considered a stupid, unthinking person, the pea hit it big with the famous nursery rhyme, "Pease porridge hot, Pease porridge cold, Pease porridge in the pot, nine days old." A word of advice: Be very careful if you drive in a pea-soup fog.

Corn originally meant any small particle, even sand or salt. That is why beef preserved by the use of salt is called corned beef.
The word *corny* was first used by vaudeville actors to describe audiences "in the sticks." To show business professionals in the early twentieth century, every town outside New York was Bridgeport, Connecticut.

By this they meant that, away from big towns, audience reactions were unsophisticated.

Since these "corn-fed" audiences relished a broad brand of humor, it became known as "corn-fed humor," a phrase that now simply means "a corny joke." And while *corny* means *old-fashioned*, it is still widely used with a fond smile.

//

Sandwiches were eaten for a long
time before they had a name, but the
sandwich as we know it was named for
Sir John Montague, the Fourth Earl
of Sandwich, First Lord of the
British Admiralty, during the
American Revolution.

//

Join me, please, as I introduce a few celebrities of culinary fame. They have become food immortal and have eaten their way into our everyday diet.

Meet Mr. Samuel Benedict, a prominent man about town in New York in the 1890s. One morning, he walked into the Waldorf-Astoria Hotel and ordered a breakfast of poached eggs, toast, and bacon served with Hollandaise sauce.

Oscar, the chef, thought it was a great combination but substituted a muffin for the toast and a slice of ham for the bacon. He christened the dish *eggs Benedict* and made Sam a gastronomic celebrity.

If you have a yen for oysters, you might have a craving for oysters Rockefeller.
This delectable dish got its name from the comment of a delighted diner at Antoine's, the celebrated New Orleans restaurant. When the patron tasted it, he said to the waiter, "The flavor of these oysters is as rich as Rockefeller." He might also have added, "The world is my oyster."

Sandwiches were eaten for a long time before they had a name, but the sandwich as we know it was named for Sir John Montague, the

Fourth Earl of Sandwich, First Lord of the British Admiralty, during the American Revolution.

The Earl of Sandwich was known as an inveterate gambler. He hated to put down his cards long enough to eat. During one of his famous round-the-clock sessions, he ordered his servant to put thick-sliced roast beef between two pieces of bread and bring it to the gambling table. Some food historians say the modern sandwich was born at exactly five a.m. on the morning of August 6, 1762. From that moment to this, two or more slices of bread with food of some kind between them immortalized the infamous Earl.

Bite into a biscuit made of whole grain flour and it's called a *graham cracker*. It's named for an American whose name became part of the language because of his ideas on diet.

Sylvester Graham was a Presbyterian minister who thought more of his congregation's stomachs than he did of their souls. He preached against the evil of drink and was convinced the nation's eating habits were equally sinful.

Graham led a crusade against gluttony at the dinner table, preached the virtues of a vegetarian diet that avoided meats and fats, and insisted that it would help people be both healthy and temperate if they gave up white bread for bread made of un-sifted whole wheat flour.

These were radical views during the time of the presidency of Andrew Jackson, when rich white bread and hearty meals were a symbol of good living. Graham was attacked in the press but the attacks only helped spread his ideas. Health faddists began forming "Graham societies." Health resorts were established in some cities, and there were shops that specialized in the sale of products Graham approved, forerunners of modern health food stores.

He was considered an eccentric by many, but he was among the first to promote health ideas that gave us graham flour, graham bread, and, of course, the famous graham cracker.

Describe someone as having a voracious appetite and you compare that person to Gargantua, a giant with such enormous eating habits he was never satisfied.

In the folk tales of medieval Europe, he was a friendly giant who went around helping people out of trouble. He was a huge, noisy fellow, peace-loving and comical, with a thirst and hunger to match his size. Similarly, French folklore gives us the Gargantuan for the giant with a prodigious appetite.

Maybe you've tasted eggs Sardou, a dish of poached eggs with artichoke hearts, anchovies, chopped ham, truffles, and Hollandaise sauce. Eggs Sardou is a specialty of Antoine's restaurant in New Orleans. It was created by owner Antoine Alciatore on the occasion of a dinner the restaurateur hosted for French playwright Victorien Sardou (1831–1908), author of a satire on America called "L'Oncle Sam."

Dame Nellie Melba, the world-famous soprano, started off in life as Helen Mitchell. Born in Australia, she adopted her professional name from the city of Melbourne and called herself "Melba." She was made a dame of the British Empire in 1918 and became known as Dame Nellie Melba.

On one of her visits to London, Dame Nellie Melba stayed at the Savoy Hotel. She was on a strict diet and ordered nothing but dry toast. The head waiter was busy and left its preparation to one of his men. Somehow things went awry, and the toast served was much too thin and dry. By the time the chef realized the error, it was too late. He rushed to Melba's table, profusely apologizing and expecting a complaint. To his surprise, Melba didn't mind at all.

To the contrary, she complimented the chef on the "exquisite toast," the likes of which she had never tasted before. The chef was overjoyed, and there and then called the toast "Melba toast." Dame Nellie also contributed another dish named for her, the famous peach Melba.

Filet of sole marguery à la Diamond Jim is a dish with a long name that pays tribute to "Diamond" Jim Brady, who was the symbol of the age of opulence.

He made his fortune selling railroad supplies, but gained his notoriety with his flashy and flamboyant style. Jim Brady also had a passion for food and he weighed 240 pounds to prove it.

While on a trip to Europe, Diamond Jim fell in love with a filet of sole dish. When he came back to the United States, he asked the restaurateur George Rector to send his son to Paris to learn how to make it. The resulting dish was filet of sole marguery à a la Diamond Jim.

The hamburger has traveled many miles since it started off as shredded raw meat called *tartar steak* that came from the Russian Baltic provinces. The Germans picked up the dish and soon the city of Hamburg, Germany, became famous for it and gave it its name. However, it was Dr. J. H. Salisbury, a food faddist, who helped make it popular in the United States, and the term *Salisbury steak* became widely known.

While Hamburg, Germany, boasted of introducing hamburger to the world, the town of Hamburg, New York, claimed that America's favorite food was invented there in the summer of 1885.

Harvard beets is a dish of beets cooked in vinegar and sugar. One explanation comes from the deep crimson color of the cooked beets, similar to the color of the jersey the Harvard football team wears.

Another theory explains the dish was conceived at a seventeenth-century English tavern called Harwood's, whose customers included a Russian immigrant. Upon immigrating to the United States, this customer opened a restaurant in Boston under the same name. The new American kept pronouncing his establishment with a name that sounded more like "Harvard" than "Harwood" and so it was that the dish he brought to this country became known as Harvard beets.

Lobster Wenberg instead of lobster Newburg should have been featured on the menus of restaurants that offer lobster dishes. But Charles Wenberg, a famous shipping magnate, made a big mistake.

He was foolish enough to annoy the great restaurateur, Lorenzo Delmonico. Wenberg had discovered the dish in South America and described it glowingly to Delmonico. Delmonico was so taken by the dish, he instructed his chef to prepare the shelled lobster in a rich sauce of sherry cream and egg yolks. He served the dish to his wealthy patrons and named it "Lobster Wenberg."

It remained on Delmonico's menu until one day Wenberg got into a fight in the restaurant's main dining room and was bodily thrown out. The next day, the name of the dish was changed. It appeared on the Delmonico menu as "Lobster Newburg."

It may have been done to honor the city on the Hudson, and it's the name it has kept to this day.

If your taste goes to Nesselrode pudding, a great dessert made of ice cream with chestnuts, fruit, and maraschino, you are paying tribute to Count Karl Robert Nesselrode (1780–1862), a Russian diplomat and statesman. His chef invented the concoction but the count enjoyed the dish so much he named it for himself.

We can thank Louis Pasteur for the germ-free pasteurized milk that we drink in safety today. We often forget, however, that his well-known discovery came out of experiments with France's national beverage: wine.

In the 1850s, the immortal French chemist first discovered that certain bacteria caused rapid "artificial" fermentation that could be prevented if the wine was exposed to high temperatures. This led to the method whereby milk and other foods could be sterilized by heating and rapid cooling.

Porterhouse steak has a long history that started way back in 1814 when a New Yorker whose name was Martin Morrison introduced the cut of meat as an item on the menu of his restaurant. The New York porterhouse was so called after the English porterhouses where porter, beer, steaks, and chops were sold.

The story of pralines goes this way: The maréchal du Plessis-Praslin César de Choiseul got heartburn one day from eating almonds but he couldn't resist them. His servant suggested that he have the chef brown the praline. Another story: The sugar-coated praline was named for Plessis-Praslin when he had his cook prepare something special for King Louis VIV, the field marshal's dinner guest one night.

More likely, pralines were invented by Plessis-Praslin's man as one of the many culinary triumphs that all chefs vied with each other to produce in the seventeenth century. At first, the dish was called *Praslins*, and in time the spelling was shortened to *pralines*. Plessis-Praslin, who put down a revolt of the nobles in 1649, may have served them pralines at his side.

Look up *Sally Lunn* in a cookbook and you may find a recipe for a muffin, a sweet bread, or a tea cake, depending on the book you use. The real Sally Lunn was a pastry cook who peddled her tea cakes from a basket in the fashionable English resort city of Bath.

Later in the eighteenth century, a baker and musician by the name of Dalmer bought her recipe, built a flourishing business, and even wrote a song about the pastry. His son made the name a catchword that was still popular when nearly a century later a Gilbert and Sullivan character in "The Sorcerer" sang about Sally Lunn.

Sirloin steak is one of the legends that has amused people for years.
It began in the seventeenth century and owes its name to King Henry VIII. His Majesty was dining on a loin of beef. He said the dish was so outstanding it should be knighted, and henceforth be called "Sir Loin."

Its true origin, however, comes from the French *surlonge*, meaning *above the loin*. Of course, there is really no reason why we shouldn't believe a king of England made this pun and acted out the dramatic scene—but we must be realistic and accept *surlonge* as the true origin of *sirloin*. In talking about sirloin, we mustn't forget the word *steak* itself. It takes its name from the way meat was cooked on a thin stake from an Old English word, *staca*, related to *stick*.

The well-known beef Stroganoff was named for the nineteenth-century Russian diplomat Count Paul Stroganoff. Joining the count with another popular dish was Arthur Wellesley, First Duke of Wellington, for whom beef Wellington was named. And along with these two dishes named for distinguished men, beef Bourguignon was named for Burgundy, France.

Tenderloin is the most tender filet of beef and often referred to by butchers as *filet mignon* and *Chateaubriand*. United States slang picked up the word to describe the police district in New York City that included most of the Broadway theaters, hotels, and other places of amusement. Gambling and graft flourished in this area. It inspired one policeman who was so happy to be transferred to the 29th district covering this territory in 1890 to say, "I've had nothing but chuck for a long time but now I'm going to get tenderloin."

Tournedos à la Rossini is a dish created by the Italian composer, Gioachino Antonio Rossini (1792–1868), best known for "The Barber of Seville" (1816). According to the story, Rossini was dining at the Café Anglais in Paris. Bored with the beef dishes on the menu, he suggested his meat be prepared in a different way. But the maître d'hôtel protested. "Never would I dare offer such a thing; it is un-presentable," he said. "Well, then, arrange for it not to be seen!" the composer answered.

Ever after, we are told, tournedos were served not before the eyes but behind the diner's back. Hence, the name in French *tourne le dos*, which means *turn your back*. There is no question that tournedos à la Rossini is considered one of the richest and most expensive dishes in the world. And here's why: The recipe includes succulent slices of fried filet of beef, set on fried bread, capped with foie gras, crowned with truffles, and coated with Périgueux sauce. This is served, of course, with Rossini's music in the background.

A famous dessert carries the name of beautiful and flamboyant Lillian Russell, who was the toast of the town from the night she made her first appearance at Tony Pastor's Opera House in Gilbert and Sullivan.

Only eighteen at the time, the singer and actress was fresh from Clinton, Iowa, where she was born Helen Louise Leonard. For the next thirty years, her beauty and talent brought her fame and fortune. They named a little town in Kansas after her, but she will best be remembered for the dessert of a half cantaloupe filled with a large scoop of ice cream that's called a *Lillian Russell*.

Lorenzo Delmonico transformed America's diet and introduced the institution of the restaurant to the United States.
He came to America at the age of nineteen and joined his two uncles in the wine and catering business. He persuaded his uncles to open New York's first restaurant catering to the upper class. It was an immediate success. Encouraged, he opened another restaurant at Broadway and 26th Street in 1876. It became a world-famous establishment and the forerunner and inspiration of the hundreds of restaurants that followed.

It was Lorenzo Delmonico who was responsible for the acceptance of the restaurant as an institution. It transformed America's social behavior as more and more Americans dined out. The social stag dinner, where men ate without the company of their wives, led to the formation of gentlemen's clubs, where the famous club sandwich was introduced.

Every American knows Delmonico's name. They mention it more than they realize. So when you dig into a properly prepared Delmonico steak, reserve one bite in tribute to Lorenzo Delmonico.

Vicomte François-René de Chateaubriand (1768–1848) was a minor nobleman who survived the turbulent years of the French Revolution. He had a colorful and varied political career. He was a Royalist at precisely the wrong time in French history. He fought on the Royalist side, was seriously wounded, recuperated, and then held minor diplomatic posts under Napoleon.

His name has lasted, however, because of the culinary creativity of his chef, who concocted a specialty he named for his employer. The Chateaubriand steak has kept his name alive for all the gourmets in the world.

If one man had to be chosen to epitomize modern gastronomy and be described as the quintessential epicurean, it would be Auguste Escoffier (1847–1935).

Escoffier was made a member of the French Legion of Honor in 1920, and was renowned as a chef and restaurateur. Author of a number of books on the art of cooking, Escoffier will live on as a culinary eponym with the creation of the famous sauce that bears his name: Escoffier sauce.

Chicken Marengo commemorated Napoleon's victory over the Austrians at Marengo in 1800.

Napoleon had moved so far ahead of his provisions, his cook had to scrape up whatever he could find in the neighborhood to feed the army. The result was a chicken dish made with tomatoes, eggs, crawfish, garlic, and oil. The combination pleased Napoleon so much that he ordered his chef to serve him the same dish after every battle. Chicken Marengo became the standard fare of Napoleon and his army.

We pay special honor to the master of them all, Marie-Antoine Carême, known as "the king of cooks and the cook of kings."

One of his crowning culinary achievements was a lavish pastry he called "Apple Charlotte" for England's Princess Charlotte. When he served Czar Alexander of Russia, he invented a custard set in a circle of ladyfingers and named it "Charlotte Russe."

Now we know how some eponymous culinary immortals have eaten their way to gastronomic fame.

A Political Menu

//

Thomas Jefferson made food news more
than once. He was the first president
to grow a tomato, and on New Year's
Day in 1802, he received 1,235 pounds
of Cheshire cheese from Cheshire,
Massachusetts, at the White House.

//

The language of politics is ever-changing. It touches a variety of subjects including sports, finance, gambling, the sea, and, of course, food. The expressions range from flavorful and spicy—to downright unappetizing.

Let's go to a barbecue that started when Spanish explorers visited Haiti and were introduced to a native dish.

It was the meat of game animals roasted over an open fire. They saw the natives build raised frames for cooking. This was done to protect the food from wild animals. The name given to this kind of raised frame was *barbacoa*. When the traveling Spaniards began to cook their meat over an outdoor fire, they called it by this new name. Later, when the word traveled to the United States, it became the well-known *barbecue*.

Politicians discovered the barbecue by 1800 and used it for political rallies. It was noticed that having a barbecue was a good way to get a large group of people to sit through a long series of dull speeches. In 1840, William Henry Harrison, the Whig candidate for president, held a mammoth political barbecue at which party workers and prospective voters consumed eighteen tons of meat. Oh yes, he won the election.

In modern times, political barbecues were given by Lyndon B. Johnson at his Texas ranch. In the early fifties, the general public picked up the idea and entertained with backyard barbecues.

Food has figured prominently in political campaigns and terms for office. Herbert Hoover called for a full dinner pan and a chicken for every American. During the Warren Harding administration, the public was very much aware of the Teapot Dome scandal. They were told it was just a fishing expedition.

Thomas Jefferson made food news more than once.

He was the first president to grow a tomato, and on New Year's Day in 1802, he received 1,235 pounds of Cheshire cheese from Cheshire, Massachusetts, at the White House. Andrew Jackson outdid Jefferson in 1837, when 1,400 pounds of cheese was delivered to Jackson's last reception in Washington. Ten thousand people attended and left the cheese and the White House in shambles. It was said that the smell of cheese lingered in the carpets and furniture for months.

Alfred Smith, the presidential candidate against FDR in 1933, gave us the famous line, "No matter how you slice it, it's still baloney." He also gave us alphabet soup, the literary broth featuring pasta shaped as letters of the alphabet. Critical of the New Deal with such agencies as the NRA, TVA, CCC, and AAA, Smith referred to it as "a bowl of alphabet soup."

Pork has been listed on the political menu since the late nineteenth century.

It has become political slang for *graft* because of its high content of fat and grease. The US Congress took over the word in "pork barrel politics" when they passed legislation designed to give funding for the benefit of states at federal government expense.

Pork barrel politics is related to the *slush fund*, which gets its name from the practice of nineteenth-century sailors who boiled large pots of pork and other fatty meats. The "slush"—or fat—was skimmed off and put into large barrels. This slush was sold, and proceeds were used for the crew's pleasure. In current political lingo, the term *slush fund* refers to hidden money used for illegal or corrupt political purposes.

The *lame duck* is an office-holder who fails to be re-elected, but whose term has not yet expired. The 27nd Amendment, limiting the president to two terms of office, made it possible for him to be a *lame duck president*, a description now used for presidents in the second half of their last term. The situation has inspired some to say he waddles through the last term in office like a wounded duck.

As for the political kitchen cabinet, President Harry S. Truman said it best: "If you can't stand the heat in the kitchen, get out." And in 1876, "fish or cut bait" was first uttered in the US Congress by Joseph Gumey Cannon, the Illinois representative.

Another fish on the political scene is the *red herring*, an expression meaning *a diversionary tactic*. In the smoking process, a herring develops a strong smell, and also changes color. When hunting was a popular activity for gentlemen, it was discovered that hounds would follow the scent of smoked herring, and such bait could divert their attention from their original pursuit.

After World War I, politicians distracted voters with talk of the threat of communism. Accusing their opponents of being soft on communism, candidates smeared their opponents with labels of "Red Menace." Even today, the red herring is used to throw voters off the scent of official wrongdoing, or to justify politicians' behavior.

A junket started out as a delicious dessert the French called *jonquette*. Nobody is quite sure how it came to mean *expeditions enjoyed by legislators at government expense*. Through the years, *junket* deteriorated to simply *junk*.

When we talk about food that has little nutritional value, we call it *junk food*. We're deluged with unsolicited advertisements called *junk mail* and a place that is littered with cheap goods is called a *junk shop*. As for *junkie*, it was first used as a slang word in 1982, when it was considered an historical verbal landmark and cultural signpost. Today, *junkie* is a standard, everyday word which has traveled a long way from its point of origin as a tasty French dessert.

//

The plum started its fortunate career as
the Old English word *plume*. Alexander
the Great brought it to Greece from
Damascus, Syria. The Romans called it
"the plum of Damascus," which became
"the damson plum" in English.

//

A mericans have eaten and talked about apples for more than 200 years.

One of the men we must thank for the apple tree's widespread presence is Jonathan Chapman, better known as Johnny Appleseed. Many people thought of Johnny as a legendary figure, but he was very alive indeed. Born in Massachusetts around 1775, Chapman set out alone into the wilderness that is now Ohio, Indiana, and western Pennsylvania. He traveled with a sack of apple seeds he had collected from cider mills, and he planted the seeds wherever he went.

The apple is now part of our everyday diet. For more than two centuries, we've eaten apple pies, apple fritters, and apple Brown Betty. Then came along apple butter, apple cobblers, apple dumplings, and apple cake. We bake them, cook them, fry them, can them, and play games with them when we bob for apples. We call them names like McIntosh, Delicious, Cortland, Gravenstein, and even Crab.

And how many times a day do we talk "apple talk"?

Nothing is more American than apple pie. And when things are in "apple pie order," they are arranged as precisely as they should be. English translators of the Bible used the word *apple* because the pupil of the eye was thought to be a solid, apple-shaped body. Since it is essential to sight, the eye's apple or pupil is cherished, and "the apple of one's eye" came to mean anything extremely precious. The Adam's apple is a little projection in the neck, and the drink applejack has been with us since colonial times.

"An apple a day keeps the doctor away" is a phrase we've all heard hundreds of times, and if you "upset the apple cart," that means you've ruined carefully laid plans. You say "the apple doesn't fall far from the tree" to explain why a person's negative trait shows up in his child. For generations, there has been the practice of giving the teacher a shiny red apple as a gift. Of course, it was nothing but a bribe with the silent prayer that the teacher would overlook any mischief of the day and forgive the "apple polisher."

Many words and phrases have been affected by this famous fruit. "The Big Apple" was a dance in the thirties, and it was New York City itself that became known as *the Big Apple*. A profound comment on the apple can be credited to William Shakespeare: "There's small choice," the bard wrote, "in rotten apples."

The apricot can be traced back to ancient Rome, where the fruit was called praecoquum, *or early ripening.*
From there, it moved into Arabic and Portuguese, eventually appearing in English as *apricock*. Modest souls of the eighteenth century sanitized the word, and it became *apricot*.

There are Biblical students who claim it was the apricot and not the apple that tempted Eve in the Garden of Eden. If that were true, would "Adam's apple" have been called "Adam's apricot"?

The cantaloupe is a melon that is round or oval, weighs two to four pounds, has orange flesh, and is known for its sweetness. Cantaloupe comes from the name of a papal villa near Rome called Cantalupo.

The name *grapefruit* has stumped scholars and agricultural experts for years. It was suggested that the word comes from *great fruit*. If so, the transition from *great fruit* to *grapefruit* probably took place immediately because it was easier to say.

The lemon is a yellow-skinned, tangy citrus fruit used in a wide variety of dishes including main courses, desserts, and drinks. The word comes from the Persian *limun*, and passed as *lemon* into English, where it is used in many different ways.

In slot machines, any combination that includes a lemon is a loser. Anything that doesn't turn out well, or an automobile that is always in for repair, is called a *lemon*. You are even protected by "lemon law," which says that if the product still contains a defect after a reasonable number of attempts to remedy it, the warrantor must permit the consumer either a refund or replacement without charge. But since some bad situations are unavoidable, we are encouraged to make the best of it. When life hands you lemons, make lemonade.

While the lemon has a negative connotation in many expressions, the peach enjoys a positive reputation. When someone is given enthusiastic approval, she is a peach. *Peach* started off in Latin as *persicum malum,* or *Persian apple.* Through the years, it became *peche,* and then ultimately *peach.*

Peaches and cream symbolized high living because cream was considered the fat of the land, and peach a most delicious fruit. In Atlanta, Georgia, natives refer to Peachtree Street, a main thoroughfare lined with elegant houses. And when the ideal of beauty is described, the woman is said to have a "peaches and cream complexion."

The plum started its fortunate career as the Old English word plume. Alexander the Great brought it to Greece from Damascus, Syria. The Romans called it "the plum of Damascus," which became "the damson plum" in English. The famous greengage plum is named for Sir William Gage, an amateur English botanist. One very special plum is the "political plum," another name for a choice political job.

The use of the word *plum* for *choice prize* comes from the famous nursery rhyme about Little Jack Horner. It was King Henry VIII of England who played an important role in Jack's fame. The ruler of England was furious when he wasn't allowed to divorce his first wife, Catherine of Aragon. In his anger, he robbed convents and monasteries, which alarmed the abbot of the Gastonbury monastery. After discussing the problem with chief steward John Horner, the abbot decided on a gesture of good will.

During the Christmas season of 1535, Horner was sent to the king with deeds to twelve estates belonging to the monastery. When Horner came back, he reported that the English ruler was pleased with the gifts but he neglected to mention the gift he stole for himself: one deed to a property. News of the theft spread. An unknown author wrote the poem about Little Jack Horner, who stuck his thumb in a Christmas pie and pulled out a plum. For several generations, *plum* was slang for

100,000 pounds. Even today, 100,000 pounds or any choice prize is still called a plum.

The pomegranate is a red, tough-skinned fruit containing many seeds and a pulpy, sour-sweet flesh. The name comes from the French *pomme*, or *apple*, plus the Latin *granatum*, meaning *many-seeded*. The pomegranate was called "the fruit of the ancient," and even today in the Eastern world, when a newly married couple enters their new home, pomegranates are broken at the doorway.

We all know the raisin as a sweet, dried grape. Raisins are eaten plain, mixed with nuts, or cooked in cakes, pastries, breads, and puddings. The raisin gets its name from the Latin *racemus*, which became *raisin* through the years. In 1873, the summer was so hot and dry that grapes dried on the vines in the California San Joaquin Valley. One enterprising grower shipped the dried grapes to a grocer friend of his in San Francisco. The grocer, who was just as enterprising, called them Peruvian delicacies for no better reason than that a Peruvian ship was in port. The promotion was such a success that it inspired the beginnings of the raisin industry.

Throw some raspberries into the fruit salad, and you're going back to ancient times when the berry grew profusely in Greece and was called the "red berry of Mount Ida."

From the English *rasp* meaning *to scrape thoroughly*, the name refers to the plant's thorny branches. As berries were removed, these branches made a scraping sound which was, perhaps, reminiscent of the insulting noise made by simultaneously sticking out the tongue and blowing.

We call this sound the "Bronx cheer," which is appropriate since it was probably started by enthusiastic baseball fans in the Bronx. This unique "cheer" gave the fans an opportunity to express their true feelings for some of the baseball players. The Bronx cheer, more properly called "the raspberry," was not considered a bad thing, according to sports psychologists. In a way, they said, "the raspberry" civilized the game because the famous sound gave fans an alternative to throwing things.

Rhubarb has long been the subject of debate as to whether it is a fruit or a vegetable. Technically, it is an herb, but since it's often used in a pie filling with a sweet sauce, many people think of it as a fruit. It grows profusely along the Volga River, the longest river in Europe.

Rhubarb became theatrical slang because a play sometimes calls for a crowd scene that has no actual written lines. When some noise is needed, the actors have traditionally been told to repeat over and over: "rhu-bar-bar, rhu-bar-bar." This repetition by many voices does well to simulate the background sounds of a crowd.

From the table to the theatre, rhubarb then moved to baseball, where it came to mean a noisy dispute between a manager and an umpire, with players joining in waving arms, kicking up dust, and slamming their hats to the ground.

//

Nobody knows the real date of this
important culinary event, but it was
a commercial baker in Naples, Italy,
who made the momentous discovery of
pizza. He found it was possible to make
a dainty pie without an upper crust.

//

One of the world's basic foods is bread, which is made from flour and water, often with the addition of yeast, salt, and other ingredients. Called "the staff of life," bread comes shaped in loaves, rolls, flat cakes, and rings. It's one of man's earliest foods.

Bread goes back to Biblical times, and the ancient expression "not by bread alone" is found in Deuteronomy 8:3. This phrase means that a person's spirit must be cared for as well as his body.

Long ago, the occupation of baker was a precarious one. Bakers were often subjected to severe penalties if they cheated their customers by short-weighing bread. In 1266, when the English Parliament passed a law imposing strict regulations regarding bread weight, bakers took no chances and made sure they followed the law.

Since it was difficult to make loaves of a uniform weight, they always added a thirteenth loaf to each shipment of twelve. This custom guaranteed there would be no shortchanging. As a result, the expression "baker's dozen" came to be known for "thirteen."

There are countless different breads we eat today, and many of them have their own stories.

Sourdough bread became associated with the Alaskan gold rush soon after 1896, and *sourdough* came to mean *prospector*. The practice of saving a lump of yeasty dough from one batch of bread to start the next can be traced to the ancient Egyptians.

Pumpernickel bread is the coarse, dark bread that carries with it the legendary story of Napoleon's aide.

He refused to eat the bread when it was offered to him in Germany. In disgust, he gave his German host his opinion: "*C'est du pain pour Nickel*," or "It is bread fit for Nickel," Napoleon's horse. *Pain pour Nickel* stuck and corrupted through the years into the name of the bread we know today as *pumpernickel*.

Anadama bread comes from a cornmeal recipe developed by a Yankee farmer whose wife Anna was too lazy to cook for him.

When a neighbor asked him what he called the bread, the old Yankee replied, "Anna, damn 'er." Another version claims that the husband was a Yankee sea captain who endearingly referred to his wife as "Anna, damn 'er." Anna's bread was delicious and would not spoil on long voyages. When his wife died, the captain is said to have written as an epitaph: "Anna was a lovely bride, but Anna, damn 'er, she up and died."

Challah is a traditional Jewish bread. It is served on the Sabbath and takes on a different shape at holiday feasts. For the Sabbath, it is braided; for Rosh Hashanah, the New Year, and for Yom Kippur, the Day of Atonement, it is rounded.

The popover is a light, hollow muffin made from an egg batter similar to that used in making Yorkshire pudding. The name *popover* comes from the fact that the batter rises and "pops over" the muffin dish while baking.

The English muffin is a round, flat muffin made from flour, yeast, malt, barley, vinegar, and farina. English muffins are usually split and toasted, then buttered and spread with jam or preserves. Americans don't make English muffins at home, preferring to buy those baked by the S. B. Thomas Company of New York.

Samuel B. Thomas emigrated from England with his mother's recipe and began making muffins at his New York bakery in 1880. That is why those round, flat breads are called *English muffins*.

The bagel is a round roll shaped like a doughnut. The "roll with a hole" came from eastern Europe and made a big hit in America. Of course, there is one thing every bagel maven knows: Bagels, cream cheese, and lox go together in a triumph of taste.

American doughnuts go back to the time of the Pilgrims, who learned to make these "nuts" of fried sweet dough in Holland before coming to the New World. The first American doughnuts didn't have holes at all. They were literally little nuts of dough.

The doughnut with the hole became nationally famous with the story of a Rockport, Maine, sea captain named Hanson Crockett Gregory. He claimed to have scooped out the soggy centers of his wife's doughnuts in 1847 so that he might slip them over the spokes of his ship's wheel, thereby being able to nibble while "keeping an even keel."

So impressed were Rockport's citizens with Gregory's contribution that they placed a plaque on his house commemorating his culinary creation.

Croissants are properly named: They are rich, flaky rolls formed in the shape of a crescent, the word for which is *croissant* in French. The rolls originated in Vienna, where chefs created them to celebrate the defeat of the Turks in 1869. Since the Turkish emblem is a crescent, the Viennese were symbolically devouring their enemies.

The scone is a small, light cake cooked in an oven or on a griddle. Many people think the name is related to the Scottish village called Scone, near Perth. They suggest there is a connection to the "Stone of Scone," a place where Scottish kings were crowned. But the scone claims no such relationship and gets its name from the Dutch word *schoonbrood*, meaning *fine bread.*

We think of toast as a brown, crisp slice of bread that has been exposed in one way or another to heat. Through the years, another meaning for the word evolved. A "toast" became a drink used as a tribute to someone who had either reached a milestone in life or made an outstanding achievement. This derived from the British custom of putting highly spiced toast in a glass of liquor, especially sherry. By doing so, they believed they improved the flavor. Eventually the toast was found to be of no real value and was left out of the drink. However, drinking to the health of a person or to a cause is still called *a toast* today.

The toastmaster at a dinner or banquet is the master of ceremonies. He introduces guests and speakers, proposes toasts, and is often expected to be prepared with a wealth of stories appropriate for the occasion. He toasts the guest of honor as the "toast of the town," asking everyone to clink their glasses. This is to ensure good health and drive away evil spirits because the devil doesn't like the sound of clinking glasses.

And remember *zwieback*? It's hard, dry toast that is popular not only for babies, but for adults as well. The word, first recorded in 1894, is German and means *twice baked.*

Nobody knows the real date of this important culinary event, but it was a commercial baker in Naples, Italy, who made the momentous discovery of pizza.
He found it was possible to make a dainty pie without an upper crust. Perhaps running short on dough, he simply sprinkled meat, cheese, and olives on top of the one crust. It was soon learned that a dish of this sort, when baked, was very tasty.

It became customary to use a pointed tool to cut indentations around the edge of the bread to make it look more appealing. Neapolitans began to call the novel dish *pizza* after the old Italian word for *point.* Pizza spread to other cities in Italy, and immigrants brought it with them to the United States. Pizza is now a full-fledged American citizen and is universally considered a favorite American dish.

Bread and *loaf* are two Old English words that were around centuries ago. In those early days, *loaf* meant *bread*, and *bread* meant *a slice of loaf.* If you wanted a piece of bread, you would have said, "Please give me a bread of loaf." In time, as more and more people asked for "a bread," the word came to mean the food, while *loaf* was used for the shape of the baked object.

In Roman times, any type of hard shell was called *crusta.* This is why hard-shelled creatures such as crabs and lobsters are called *crustaceans.*

The word *crusta* traveled from Latin to French, and it entered English as *crust.* Bakers of olden times took great pride in their ability to make a thick, hard crust. The soft bread inside was usually called the *crumb.* Sometimes the crumbs stayed fresh for a long while, but when they didn't, it was unappetizing and "crummy." *Crummy* thus came to describe something worthless, shabby, cheap, and inferior.

If your friends are the "upper crust," you are mingling with wealthy or influential people who are members of a high social class.
Long ago, it was considered proper etiquette to slice off and present the king or the ranking nobleman with the upper crust of a loaf of bread. This ritual symbolized the importance of being one of the elite, especially if one had the "dough." The slang word *dough* in the sense of *money* goes back to the 1850s, and can be used interchangeably with *mazuma, jac, do-re-mi, gravy, wampum,* or just the ordinary *buck.*

What better way to describe a friend than to say he is one with whom we break bread?

//

In Ireland, the pot of hospitality always
hung over the open fire, ready to be
dipped into by any unexpected visitor.
What it tasted like, however, was a
matter of pot luck.

//

There are few words that have gained more coverage in our everyday conversation than the three-letter word *pot.*

We use a coffee pot, a teapot, a flower pot, and a jam pot all the time—and sometimes all at the same time. We cook in a pot on a pot-bellied stove and talk about a portly man as having a pot belly. A pot boiler is a literary piece merely to make a living for the author and keep the pot boiling.

However in the Middle Ages, things were quite different. Since there were no fancy cuts of beef for the peasants, most of their meals came from tossing leftovers into great iron pots left simmering over the fire. Oftentimes, they didn't know what they were going to eat, so when they invited a visitor to take *pot luck,* it was a matter of luck as to what was in the pot and whether there would be enough to go around. In Ireland, the pot of hospitality always hung over the open fire, ready to be dipped into by any unexpected visitor. What it tasted like, however, was a matter of pot luck.

The famous expression known as "the pot calling the kettle black" is used to describe anyone who blames another for faults which he also has.

This seventeenth-century phrase is based on the fact that pots and kettles would both be blackened like any other cooking utensils after long use over an open fire. "He has gone to pot" is an expression that dates back to Elizabethan times, when pieces of meat were chopped up and put into a pot for a stew. They were usually inferior pieces of meat, the kind rich men trimmed off and gave to the servants for their stew pot. "Going to the pot" came to mean going down in the world when someone lost his social position and was thus described as "gone to pot."

And still the "potty" words go on. Pot cheese is a cottage cheese. Pot of gold is an imaginary reward. Pot roast is a piece of meat cooked slowly. Pot can mean marijuana, and a pothead is the person who smokes it. Potage is a thick soup. A pot is a dropped goal in rugby football. Pot-au-feu is a large cooking pot familiar in France, and pot valor is another name for Dutch courage or "whiskey courage" inspired by alcohol.

Right now we'll sweeten the pot and put it on the back burner, and hope we won't go from the frying pan into the fire.

///

It was in the Eastern world that Marco
Polo found the aromatic seasoning
ginger, and the European appetite for
condiments made it a treasured spice.
From the Old English word *gingifer*, the
hot, pungent spice gave rise to the word
gingerly, meaning *delicately*.

///

People often enjoy a nice spicy story—so here's one about the housewives of England.

More than a century ago, they would ask merchants for an aromatic seasoning they called *allspice*. This pungent spice wasn't known in Europe before the discovery of the West Indies. English ladies thought the seeds combined all the tasteful flavors of cinnamon, cloves, and nutmeg, and described this flavorful mélange as "allspice."

American housewives joined their English cousins in following recipes that made generous use of spices. Since there was no refrigeration, however, spices were most often used to cover up off-flavors in meat. As a result, they were always in demand in the general stores, and Yankee ship owners made great profit importing them. Elihu Yale made his fortune selling spices, especially pepper, and later his wealth was used to start Yale University.

Pepper played a role during the siege of Valley Forge.
Morale among the troops dropped lower and lower as supplies of food dwindled in both quality and quantity. George Washington sent for his chief cook and insisted that some tasty dish be prepared. The cook was eager to comply, but he explained he had absolutely nothing left except a few peppercorns. "Use them," Washington commanded. That night, weary, cold, and hungry men ate tripe seasoned with peppercorns. There's nothing like pepper to make one feel peppy.

Back in Roman times, salt was scarce and expensive. Salt money was given to the Roman soldiers and was called *salarium*. When the English-speaking world needed a word to mean *regular pay*, the old Roman word for *salt money* came up and became *salary*. That is why it is sometimes said of a man, "Why, he isn't even worth his salt."

And, oh—if you should spill salt, you'd better hurry and throw a pinch of it over your left shoulder. The hope is that you will throw it in the devil's face and avoid any bad luck that comes from wastefully spilling precious salt. One tradition has it that good spirits stand behind a person's right shoulder, bad spirits behind his left. Thus, a few grains of salt tossed over the left will hit the bad spirit's eyes and distract him from the evil he might be planning.

When you take a comment "with a grain of salt," you're saying it must be "seasoned" a little in order for you to swallow it. It's another way of saying that, in your opinion, the statement is unfounded or grossly exaggerated. The expression started in ancient times when salt was thought to have magical powers. People sprinkled it on food they suspected might be poisonous, and so it became customary to eat a questionable dish only when salt was added.

The ancient superstition has disappeared, but it left a mark on the language. When we're not sure of the accuracy of a statement we, like the suspicious Romans of ancient times, are apt to say, "Take that statement *cum grano salis*—with a grain of salt."

I guess it's time to go back to the salt mines.

This is a mythical place used to refer to the workplace. The expression came from the fact that political prisoners in Russia were sent to the salt mines of Siberia for manual labor. And if you were around in the fifteenth century, you would talk a great deal about the salt cellar. There was a custom at the time to set a huge salt cellar in the middle of the table. If you were placed "above the salt" at the dinner table, you were considered an honored guest; if you were "below the salt," you sat at a lower end of the table among those considered by the host to be less important.

Salt is prevalent in everyday conversation. We talk about salt-free diets. We have salt-filled oceans, and we sometimes weep salty tears. We try to salt away our money, and we use a salt shaker or a salt spoon at meals. We speak of old salts, the crusty oldsters who live beyond their salad days. And "rubbing salt on your wounds" is another way to express "adding insult to injury."

It was in the Eastern world that Marco Polo found the aromatic seasoning ginger, and the European appetite for condiments made it a treasured spice.

From the Old English word *gingifer*, the hot, pungent spice gave rise to the word *gingerly*, meaning *delicately*. It also inspired a phrase from the seamier side of horse racing. Unscrupulous trainers would "ginger up" a horse before racing by inserting a preparation of powdered ginger into the animal's rectum. The burning, stinging sensation would make it run faster.

Ginger flavors a variety of well-loved treats, such as the ginger snap, a cookie made from ginger and molasses. The "snap" part of the cookie comes from the German *snappen*, meaning *to seize quickly*. There's ginger ale, a carbonated beverage—or perhaps you would prefer ginger beer, a mild alcoholic drink. Gingerbread, known as one of the oldest of all sweet cakes, has become a holiday tradition in the form of gingerbread men and elaborate gingerbread houses.

We all know that sesame is an edible seed, a food used for seasoning or, if squeezed, a source of oil. It must have been a familiar plant in the area of the Forty Thieves, because it was a key word in one of the stories of *The Arabian Nights*.

Ali Baba, the principal character, overheard the thieves' password, "Open sesame." Pronouncing the magical phrase, he opened the stone door to the cave where the loot was stored, and helped himself. His brother Kassim later extorted the password from him and entered the dungeon to rifle it, but was trapped when he forgot the magical words. The thieves returned, found Kassim, and killed him. Today, "open sesame" has come to signify the magical charm that makes certain people always welcome in a particular place.

In the middle of the nineteenth century, Sir Marcus Sandys, a British nobleman, came back to England after a long stay in India. Sir Marcus was a gourmet of impeccable taste. During his years in India, he developed a taste for a tangy sauce, a blend of spices and seasonings which was doused on many Indian dishes.

He brought the recipe back to his estate in Worcester, England, and commissioned two chemists, John Lea and William Perrins, to prepare bottles of the sauce for his own use and as gifts for friends. Its popularity spread, and the sauce was manufactured under the name of Worcester. It appeared in America as Worcestershire sauce, Worcestershire being the county seat of Worcester. Americans love the sauce even though the name isn't always pronounced correctly.

//

Molasses is a sweetener made from refined sugar, sugar beets, and even sweet potatoes. Molasses started its sweet life from the Latin word *mel* for *honey.*

//

How about it, sugar? Let's talk "sweet talk" as we discuss one of the sweetest subjects in the world: sugar.

One of the earliest references to sugar goes back to a report by an officer who traveled with Alexander the Great to India in the fourth century. "There is," he said, "a reed which yields honey without the help of bees." And so it was that people discovered a way to satisfy their sweet tooth.

Sugar was cultivated in India and then traveled to Asia and North Africa. Christopher Columbus's mother, who had a sugar plant on the island of Medeira, gave him a cutting to bring with him to the New World.

There are many types of sugar, including cane, beet, maple, and corn. The human desire for the sweet stuff finds expression in our everyday conversation.

The object of our affection is likely to be sweetheart, honey, sugarplum, and sweetie pie. Since the mid-nineteenth century, *sugar* has meant money, and lots of sugar has made it possible to enjoy "la dolce vita," or "the sweet life." And any man getting on in years and well-padded with cash can become a sugar daddy to a sweet young thing.

We sugarcoat words to make them sound more pleasant, and we eat food that is sugarless because of fewer calories.

Now, sweet potato, we call your attention to a sugar-coated pill that goes back to the Civil War creation of delicious drug dosages by Philadelphia pharmacist J. William R. Warner. His sugar-coated pill brought him blessings and money galore. A sweet success story if there ever was one.

And here's the sweet story of an Englishman who turned his energies to one of the hottest commodities then being handled: sugar.
When Henry Tate was sixty back in 1879, he perfected a way to compress sugar cubes that were easily handled and yet melted quickly. This discovery gave him a top spot in Europe's sugar industry.

With the fortune he made from sugar cubes, he purchased paintings by British artists and formed a discriminating collection of paintings. In his old age, he offered his art collection to England. Many collectors turned up their noses in disgust, and they wrote newspaper columns denouncing "a maker of sugar cubes who is seeking publicity."

Today, the Tate Gallery in London ranks with the best art galleries in the world and is visited by more than a million people each year. It is called the sweetest art collection in the world.

And how about honey, honey?
Honey is the sweet liquid produced by bees from flower nectar. Hon-

ey's name came from an Old English word, *hunig*, and was the first and most widespread sweetener used.

Honey has long been used as a term of endearment. The honeymoon is a period of sweet joy when the bride and groom drink a glass of mead, which is wine made with honey, every night of the first month of marriage because of its legendary powers as an aphrodisiac. There are those who say the moon has nothing to do with the marriage. They say the real word is *honeymonth*, the first month after the wedding, a time of joy and sweetness. It is also said by others that the honeymoon is soon over, honey.

Pour maple syrup over French toast or a johnnycake, and we call your attention to the syrup that dates back to the American pioneers, who learned from the Indians how to make it.
However, it was the Quaker movement that played an important role in making maple syrup popular. Since the Quakers started an organized movement in the United States to condemn slavery, they flatly refused to buy, sell, or use any commodity made with slave labor. Sugar was high on the list of such items because most of it came from the cane fields of the deep South.

As for the johnnycake, Johnny's name was added to the cake accidentally. When early pioneers discovered that this special cake of cornmeal was a delicious food, it seemed ideally suited to being carried in a saddle bag and eaten on a journey. Its real name in those early days was *journeycake*. Through the years, it became *johnnycake* because it's easier to say.

Molasses is a sweetener made from refined sugar, sugar beets, and even sweet potatoes. Molasses started its sweet life from the Latin word *mel* for *honey.*

Molasses used to be called *long sweetening,* while a less refined variety was called *short sweetening.* The darkest and least refined is called *blackstrap* or *mother liquor.* Molasses pours very slowly from its container and so it is quite natural to call someone who doesn't move very quickly "as slow as molasses."

Well, sugar, we hope all this sweet talk will bring you sweetness and light, honey!

The
Pungent
Accompaniment

II

If you've ever wondered how the little

red cranberry became as famous as

it is, take a ride down to Cape Cod,

Massachusetts. That cranberry sauce

we enjoy so much started off as crane

berries because cranes living near the

cranberry bogs ate the berries.

II

What about all those extras that go with a meal? Can you think of a hamburger without ketchup, mustard, or relish? Turkey without cranberries? A sandwich without mayonnaise?

All these accompaniments give color and dash to what might otherwise be ordinary food. Think about ketchup, also called *catsup*. The word comes from the Chinese *ket-tsiap*, which is a pickled fish sauce. English sailors picked it up in the seventeenth century. However, it wasn't until American sailors added tomatoes from Mexico to the condiment that ketchup was born and the tangy blend was picked up by pickle king Henry J. Heinz.

As for the way it's spelled, if you say *ket-tsiap* fast several times, you can hear just how it starts to sound like *ketchup*.

If you've ever wondered how the little red cranberry became as famous as it is, take a ride down to Cape Cod, Massachusetts. That cranberry sauce we enjoy so much started off as crane berries because cranes living near the cranberry bogs ate the berries.

The legend of the cranberry bogs goes like this: Many years ago, there was an argument between an Indian medicine man and Reverend Richard Bourne. The medicine man cast a spell on the reverend and trapped him in quicksand. The two men finally decided to settle their differences. They agreed to a fifteen-day marathon battle of wits. Reverend Bourne was at a decided disadvantage. He wasn't able to move, and was only kept alive by a white dove that fed him a succulent wild berry from time to time. The medicine man tried to cast a spell on the dove but couldn't do it.

At last, the medicine man fell to the ground. Exhausted from his own lack of food and water, he released Reverend Bourne from the spell. In the course of these events, one of the wild berries fell to the ground and took root. And this is how the wild cranberry bogs began. The next time you drive down to Cape Cod, cross the Bourne bridge, and pass a town called Bourne, think of Reverend Bourne because he—along with the medicine man—gave us cranberry sauce, cranberry juice, and all other succulent cranberry dishes that started off being known as crane berries.

Looking for some mustard for your hot dog?

Mustard has been around since ancient times. Mustard seeds are very fine and they're often mixed with a liquid. The word *mustard* comes from the French, who mixed the crushed seeds with *must*, a fermented wine. You can understand now how difficult it is to "cut the mustard." This popular American expression means that someone doesn't come up to expectations or achieve some desired goal. One explanation tells us the beginning of the expression was a mispronunciation of *muster* in the sense of a military review, and that to cut the mustard was to pass inspection.

Another explanation is offered. Since mustard seeds are very tiny, cutting them is no small accomplishment. It requires great care and concentration, and the job is a slow and painstaking one. But since mustard seed is usually ground to a powder, there is no reason to introduce mustard seed-cutting as a job that requires great skill. The expression "he can't cut it" is older than "cut the mustard," but the way our language sometimes works, the mustard might have been added later for rhythm or just for fun.

Talk about a famous salad dressing, and the first word that comes to mind is mayonnaise.

Mayonnaise started at the Mediterranean seaport city of Port Mahon, when it was occupied by the British. The story goes back to 1756 when a French military commander, Louis François, was hungry after battle. He ordered a meal and was annoyed it was taking so long to prepare. Frustrated, the commander stormed into the kitchen. He took whatever food he could find, put it in a pot, mixed it all together, and topped it with what looked like a yellow cream.

True or not, the story spread everywhere in Paris, and the chefs in the French capital wanted to honor the noble deeds of the commander at Port Mahon. They devised a beaten-together dressing they called mahonnaise. Mahonnaise later became the dressing we use all the time, known today as mayonnaise.

I think you'll agree that there's nothing like a pickle to give food that extra special taste.

The word *pickle* came from a Dutch fisherman, William Beukelz, who is credited with inventing the pickling process used in England as early as 1440. By the time the eighteenth century rolled around, any preserved food item was called a pickle. It was the cucumber that led the parade of other vegetables being pickled, with the most popular known as the dill pickle.

In America, pickled food was introduced by Henry J. Heinz who offered fifty-seven varieties for sale to the public. The pickle entered language in many ways. If you were in a pretty pickle, you were in trouble. *In de pikel zitten* is a Dutch phrase that means to sit in the salt solution used for preserving pickles. Certainly an uncomfortable position to be in! Just the thought of it is enough to make one go out and get pickled.

I hope you are reading all this with relish, which is any of a variety of spicy, often pickle-based condiments served as a side dish or spread on a food item. The word *relish* came to us from the French word *reles,* meaning *scent, taste,* or *aftertaste.* The Oxford English Dictionary tells us that *relish* is a great liking or enjoyment. How true!

Please pass the gravy! It's a phrase we hear often at the dinner table. What better accompaniment is there to meat, poultry, and other foods? The word *gravy* comes from the Old English word *gravey.* In America, the term *gravy* is used to explain a way of making money with little or no effort. In the 1920s, railroad men invented the expression "to ride the gravy train" to describe a run on which there was good pay and little work. The word came into general speech meaning "to be able to get a soft job that pays well."

///

What is more American than cookies in

a cookie jar just waiting for little fingers

to sneak a few? The cookie, however,

isn't really American at all, but was

borrowed from the Dutch

word *koekje*, meaning *little cake*.

///

"Just deserts" are proper punishment for an offense. How can we explain that someone who gets his just deserts should get a delicious dessert as a punishment? It's complicated to be sure, but right now you're about to go on a dessert binge. Have a great time. You deserve it.

Please taste *baba au rhum*, a fruity, delightful cake that literally means "little old woman with rum."

The word *baba* is borrowed from the Poles and means *grandmother*. This little lady baked sweet pungent breads that were an important part of the American-Polish cuisine. The one called *babka* has become an important part of American baking tastes. *Baba* is closely related to *babka* because she is the one who introduced *babka* in the first place. And who knows, while grandma made *babka*, she might have worn a *babushka*, or kerchief, on her head.

How about a piece of cake?
A cake is a baked confection that usually contains flour, butter, eggs, and a sweetener. The word *cake* comes from the Norwegian word *kaka*, which moved into English as *cake*. The cake occupies an important position in the celebration of special events in our lives such as birthdays, anniversaries, and more. The cake has also eaten its way into our everyday conversation.

"A piece of cake" is an expression often said to show how easy things are to do. We shrug off a job to do by describing it as a piece of cake. The phrase was included in a glossary of Royal Air Force slang during World War II. A successful bombing mission that took a few or no losses was called *a piece of cake*.

And when you "take the cake," you've been given a prize or an honor. The phrase comes from the "cake walk," a dance that originated in the American South.

The cake walk got its name from the fact that a strutting contest was held among the men during picnics and church box suppers. The man who strutted the best was given his choice of cakes, and the girl who baked the winner's selection became his partner. The dance was very popular during the early part of the twentieth century and accounts for some of the fancy steps in a tap dancer's routine. Couples would walk in a circle around the cake and the most graceful couple on the floor would take the cake.

"Let them eat cake!" was reported to have been said by Marie Antoinette, the extravagant, pleasure-loving queen of Louis XVI of France.

The queen did not enjoy good press in the history books. Her lack of tact and discretion in dealing with the Paris proletariat is legendary. She is supposed to have uttered the famous phrase "let them eat cake" in answer to a beggar's plea for food.

Yes, it's a piece of cake talking about cake, but before we finish every last crumb, let's explain that pound cake was so named because early recipes called for a pound each of flour, sugar, butter, and eggs. It was popular and easy to make even before the days of measuring cups.

Let us not forget a cake of soap—and how anything covered with a substance stuck to the surface is "caked" with dirt.

For centuries, babies have been entertained with the nursery rhyme "pat-a-cake, pat-a-cake, baker's man," and nobody will argue with the fact that you can't have your cake and eat it, too.

What is more American than cookies in a cookie jar just waiting for little fingers to sneak a few?

The cookie, however, isn't really American at all, but was borrowed from the Dutch word *koekje*, meaning *little cake*. *Cookie* came into the language from the Dutch settlers of New York. There were several spellings for it at the beginning: *cookey, cooky,* and *cookie*—and *cookie* won out. The choice of cookies is wide and vast but one of the most unusual is the fortune cookie.

The cookie with a fortune inside was invented in 1918 by David Jung, a Chinese immigrant who had established the Los Angeles Hong Kong Noodle Company. Jung got the idea after noticing how bored people were while waiting for their orders in Chinese restaurants. He employed people to write thousands of classic fortunes, such as "Your feet shall walk upon a plush carpet of contentment." Today, fortune cookies are still served at the end of a meal in a Chinese restaurant.

And when you crack one of those cookies open, well, that's how the cookie crumbles.

I don't know how one describes pudding. Do you call it a dessert more like a pie, or more like a cake?

Whatever it is, it was an early American dessert made of boiled hasty pudding cornmeal served with milk or molasses. It was called *corn-meal mush* or *hasty pudding*. The only way to truly test how good these puddings are is to taste them. It must have tasted mighty good to Harvard men, because they called their literary society the Hasty Pudding Club way back in 1795. It points out that although something might appear to be tasty, you never really know because the proof of the pudding is in the eating.

Well, sweetie pie, I am happy to give you a piece of the pie as we talk about how one of America's favorite desserts got started.

It happened at the end of the eighteenth century when the bird now called *magpie* was shortened to simply *pie*. This bird had unusual habits. It was a collector, and it wasn't unusual to find a pie's nest filled with pebbles, pieces of broken glass, string, chicken feathers, and more. At some unrecorded time, one inspired housewife thought of placing a crust around a small pot of stew. She used whatever ingredients she had on hand—meat, fowl, or fish, plus a few vegetables. Her family liked the strange combination of food. Looking around for a name for this concoction, they compared it with a pie's nest, which was filled with a variety of odds and ends.

At that moment, a new dish called *pie* was born. The word came to include many varieties of pie: There is no other language that has a word remotely related to this English name for one of the most popular desserts.

Shoofly pie is an open pie filled with a mixture of brown sugar and molasses. The sweetness of the filling attracted flies. Pennsylvania Dutch housewives who created the dish would say, "Shoo, fly!"

Pumpkin pie, one of the first typical New England dishes, was served at the Pilgrims' second Thanksgiving in 1623. Apple pie has been an American favorite since the 1760s. We keep things in apple pie order as we keep our finger in the pie and select favorites like blueberry, peach, lemon meringue, and rhubarb, along with pie à la mode. All of them are delicious and nice as pie.

Yes, cutie pie, it's easy as pie to talk about pie in the sky, and I'm willing to give you a piece of the pie if you avoid getting pie-eyed.

I'm sure you've wondered: What's short about strawberry shortcake, the famous dessert made with pastry, strawberries, and whipped cream?

The name comes from its being made "short," meaning "crisp." In English, *shortcake* usually meant *shortbread*, which is usually crisp and a traditional specialty of Scotland. In America, however, shortcake was a rich pastry enclosing fruits. By the mid-1800s, strawberry shortcake became one of America's favorite desserts.

The dessert now known as Jell-O made its first appearance on the culinary scene when a patent for a gelatin dessert was taken out by Peter Cooper, a patron of the arts and sciences. The product didn't "make it." Nobody seemed to be interested in the "shivering pudding."

Fifty years later, Pearl B. Wait, a cough medicine manufacturer in LeRoy, New York, became bored with the cough medicine business and looked around for a new field. He came across Cooper's invention and started production on an adaptation of Cooper's gelatin dessert. The name Jell-O was coined by Wait's wife, Mary. It was suggested the dessert reminded Mary of jelly—and "O" was then a popular ending for the names of new food products.

Wait sold the business two years later for $450 to his neighbor, Francis Woodward, who had just founded a company for the manufacture of a cereal beverage he called "Grain-O." The first year, Woodward didn't do any better than Wait. One day, as he walked through the plant with his superintendent, A. S. Nico, they stopped in front of a storage section piled high with unsold cases of Jell-O. Woodward turned to his companion and said, "I'll sell you the whole Jell-O business for thirty-five dollars." Nico replied, "Thanks a lot but no thanks."

Shortly after, Woodward had cause to rejoice and Nico to weep. At the turn of the century, the long-neglected dessert suddenly caught on with the public and Jell-O is now one of the best known and most popular foods in the United States.

II

The legend of how coffee was discovered
tells of an Ethiopian shepherd who
noticed his sheep stayed up all night
when they ate certain berries. He
decided to try them himself and found
the berries had the same effect on him.

II

Haow about a cup of tea? Tea has joined American life in so many ways.

We still go to tea parties where tea roses add a decorative touch. Tea sandwiches are arranged on a tea cloth with dishes set on a tea trolley. The tea is taken from a tea caddy, which is a small box for storing tea. A *teetotaler* preaches total abstinence from alcoholic beverages, urging everyone to "be tea drinkers totally." He can sometimes create a tempest in a teapot, making a big fuss over something unimportant.

The story of tea goes back so far that its true beginning is lost in time.

According to legend, Chinese Emperor Shen Nung was known as "the Divine Healer." Nobody knew the causes of illness in those days, but the wise emperor observed that people who boiled their drinking water enjoyed good health. His servants made a fire from the branches of a nearby tree, and set a pot of water on it. As the water began to boil, some of the leaves of the branches fell into the boiling pot. "What an aroma!" said the emperor as the fragrance of the tea floated on the air for the first time. As he sipped the steaming liquid, he added, "And what a flavor!" The Chinese will tell you that this is how tea was discovered around 2737 BC.

The people of India tell another story about the origin of tea as a drink. About a thousand years ago, a saintly Buddhist priest named Darma wanted to prove his faith. He decided to do so by spending seven years without sleep, thinking only of Buddha. For five years, Darma thought of Buddha day and night. Then, to his dismay, he found himself falling asleep, and fought to keep his eyes open. In desperation, he snatched a handful of leaves from a nearby bush and chewed them, hoping they would keep him awake. They were the leaves of the tea bush. Darma felt refreshed and awake after eating them. With their help, he was able to complete seven years of meditation without once falling asleep.

The first patent for an individual tea bag was granted in 1896 to an Englishman named A. V. Smith, and until 1904, everyone drank hot tea, even in warm weather.

That year, Englishman Richard Blechynden visited the International Exposition in St. Louis, Missouri. He set up his own booth and tried to sell English tea to Americans, but he forgot to consider one thing: The temperature was so high that nobody was interested in drinking a hot beverage that would make them feel more uncomfortable. Blechynden was about ready to give up.

One evening, at the time he usually prepared to close his booth, he dumped a quantity of crushed ice into a big urn of tea. He tasted it and, to his amazement, he found the beverage to be delicious. He promptly switched to selling "iced tea" and launched a new food fashion.

Legend has it that Americans switched from tea to coffee the morning after the Boston Tea Party.

They rebelled against King George III because he refused to rescind the tea tax in 1770. Tea finally regained the lead in the 1790s because it was cheaper than coffee. Tea certainly left its imprint on American history as being one of the most important ingredients in the brewing of the American Revolution.

Today, coffee is very much a part of American life. We drink it and socialize with it, and it has become part of our everyday life and language. Americans drink coffee with breakfast, in the middle of the morning at coffee break, at lunch, and with or after dinner. We drink coffee black or lightened by cream and milk; we like it with or without sugar; and we choose caffeine or decaf, brewed or instant.

The legend of how coffee was discovered tells of an Ethiopian shepherd who noticed his sheep stayed up all night when they ate certain berries. He decided to try them himself and found the berries had the same effect on him.

In 1550, coffee reached Constantinople, moved on to Europe, and the first European coffee house was opened in Rome in 1615. The Italians have been perfecting their own way with coffee ever since. The climax of their experiments was the famous cappuccino, the coffee named after the Capuchin monks.

In the late 1880s, two of the most famous American coffee companies helped to make us a nation of coffee drinkers.

In 1878, Caleb Chase and James Sanborn, owners of coffee businesses in New England, joined forces and produced the first coffee in a sealed can. Ever since stores began to sell their one- and two-pound cans of coffee, the name *Chase and Sanborn* has been a household phrase.

Maxwell House Coffee came about from the experiments of Joel Cheek in Nashville, Tennessee. It took about two years of full-time work to develop a coffee that suited his taste. Maxwell House, a well-known hotel in Nashville, agreed to serve his blend. The guests all said it was the best coffee they had ever tasted. Later, Theodore Roosevelt was served a cup of Maxwell House coffee. When asked if he would like another cup, he answered, "Delighted. It's good to the last drop." And a slogan was born.

I invite you to a **kaffeeklatsch.**

Klatschen is a German word that means *to gossip*. So a *kaffeeklatsch* is a gossip session at which coffee is served. It all started in the early 1880s to describe a gathering of German burgher wives. The men who coined the word disapproved of their wives openly sharing thoughts with other women. They considered this activity wifely disobedience. German women of the time did not necessarily talk about women's rights per se, but they were fighting for their own recognition. Women throughout Europe began to compete for their rightful place in society, and they started the battle with *kaffeeklatsches*.

If a full cup is too much, you might prefer demitasse. It's a small cup of coffee, and it means "half a cup." Or, another option is decaffeinated coffee.

Millions of Americans who drink decaf have a European to thank for its discovery. For years, Dr. Luwig Roselius, head of a large European coffee business, had searched for a way to remove caffeine from coffee without harming the drink's flavor or aroma. And then one day in 1903, it happened.

A shipload of coffee consigned to him was deluged with sea water during a storm. The cargo was unfit for commercial sale, and Dr. Roselius decided the only thing he could do was dump the coffee. A colleague of his suggested that, before getting rid of the cargo, he turn it over to researchers for experimental purposes. One important discovery developed: Sea-washed coffee beans reacted differently from the normal coffee beans previously tested. This suggested a different approach to the problem of removing caffeine, which led to a new series of experiments.

Thus began the process used today, the same technique which removes ninety-seven percent of caffeine without affecting the delicate coffee flavor. Dr. Roselius didn't know what to call his coffee, and decided on a contraction of the French phrase meaning *without coffee*. He called it *sanka*.

You Said a Mouthful

//

Brunch is considered quite modern, but
it really started in the late 1800s as the
"company breakfast." It was a stylish
way of entertaining in literary
and artistic circles.

//

We're going to throw in everything but the kitchen sink. In other words, we're going to give you a hodge-podge, a mish-mash, a smorgasbord of stories relating to anything and everything *food*.

In the kitchen, we meet the *chef de cuisine*, the *head of the kitchen*. He might serve a meal *à la carte*, or *by the card*, referring to food items, each having its own separate price. In contrast is *table d'hote*, a term lifted directly from the French for *host's table*. Originally this meant a common table set for the guests at a hotel or other eating place. Today, *table d'hote* describes a complete restaurant meal served *prix fixe*, or at *a specified price*.

Table is used in a variety of expressions. If one lays his cards on the table, he gives it to you straight, or "straight from the shoulder." If one tables his objections, he puts off discussing them. And when the tables are turned, conditions are reversed. Then there's money received under the table, which isn't above-board because it's not reported on a tax return.

Of course, it's most important to remember our table manners: These were devised to prevent elbows from offending fellow diners or intruding on their territory. We also have the table knife and tablespoon, as well as table linens and table mats. If one drinks too much at the dinner table, he runs the risk of being "under the table."

Whether you cook from a receipt or a recipe, it makes no difference at all. Today, the terms have the same meaning. Both come from the Latin *recipere*, meaning *to receive*. The apron, which one wears to protect clothing during food preparation, comes from the French *naperon*, a small cloth or tablecloth.

A famous American expression came about because many wives controlled the purse strings of the family and made important decisions in which their husbands played no part. Such men who did just as they were told were said to be "hen-pecked" and "tied to their wives' apron strings." It was also said that some male children, even as adults, were dominated by their mothers, or "tied to their mothers' apron strings."

A meal is thought of as the time during which food is eaten. Whether it be in the morning, midday, or evening, we call it *mealtime*. A person who is the source of income for an individual or family is called a *meal ticket*. The mealy-mouthed person has his own history that started with the Greek phrase *meli muthos*, meaning *honey speech*. This refers to a person who "honey-mouthed" or "velvet-tongued" the language and, through the years, insincere "sweet-talkers" came to be known as mealy-mouthed.

Brunch is considered quite modern, but it really started in the late 1800s as the "company breakfast." It was a stylish way of entertaining in literary and artistic circles. *Brunch* came into the language when it was used to describe a combined breakfast and lunch.

If you were invited to a banquet in the seventeenth century, you would be entertained most graciously by Italian hosts from well-established families.

One of those hosts introduced a new custom: After the main course, he took guests away from the table for dessert. From then on, guests went outdoors or into another room, sitting on benches or *banchetta* to nibble delicacies. The word *banchetta* came to be associated with any type of feast, and eventually became our familiar *banquet*.

It is a far cry from the banquet to the brown-bag luncheon. This popular term usually describes a lunch packed in a paper bag and eaten at work or en route somewhere. Brown bags started their career in Pennsylvania. In 1870, there was a machine that made paper into a flat-bottomed bag that was picked up by the food industry. Today, millions of Americans "brown bag it" for lunch.

You've heard the expression "there's no such thing as a free lunch." But there used to be!

At the end of the nineteenth century, saloon customers could receive a midday meal free of charge if they drank more beer or spirits. The practice began in a restaurant in the New Orleans French Quarter. It was designed for business clientele who couldn't get home in time for lunch. The management tried to stop it, but by that time it had become so popular that it was a practice in restaurants across the country.

In those early days, free lunch consisted of a full-course meal. By the middle of the twentieth century, however, it had dwindled to a complimentary snack of pretzels, potato chips, or other cocktail nibbles.

Another common restaurant practice is leaving a tip for service. The word *tip* came from the initial letters of the phrase "to insure promptness."

In English inns and coffeehouses, it was customary to have money boxes to benefit waiters. "To insure promptness" or "to insure prompt service" was printed on the boxes. This was a reminder that depositing a coin would bring excellent results in the way of special services.

The word *grub*, a slang term for any kind of food, is often heard in the American West among cowboys, ranchers, miners, and loggers.

It's an Old English word meaning *to dig* and suggests a person who had to dig for food. Its current slang sense has been around for a couple of centuries. A more refined word is *cuisine*, which originally meant *kitchen* in French. Parisians extended its meaning to include *cookery*—and so have we.

A votre santé is one of the most familiar and oldest French drinking toasts, dating back to the eighteenth century. It means simply *to your good health*. And by the way, *yummy* comes from *yum yum*, which imitates the sound of smacking the lips. Naturally, it means *delicious* and *delectable*.

When you use flour, you're going back to the time of England's Queen Elizabeth, when her subjects used the word *flower* as a poetic expression for *the best*.

It was applied to merchandise, weapons, animals, and even people who were considered superior. Millers of the period ground wheat by a crude process, then sifted their meal. Only the finest of it passed through the cloth sieve. This top-quality ground wheat was reserved for nobility, and was called *flower of wheat*. When the poetic language of Old English lost its charm, *flower of wheat* became ordinary, plain *flour*.

The Medici family, which directed the destiny of the city of Florence from the fifteenth century until the eighteenth, did much good and much evil. Their involvement ranged from patronage of the arts to political torture and poisoning. Family members were prone to dispose of each other by assassinations led by Queen Catharine of France.

She was also rumored to give poisonous drinks to her enemies under the guise of friendship. She would serve the poison in a thick drink of gruel, or a cooked, thin cereal. One might assume that Queen Catharine's poisonings inspired the expression "to get one's gruel," except that the phrase was unknown until some 200 years after she died. Happily, eating gruel today is not such a grueling experience.

A nut is a fruit consisting of a hard or tough shell around an edible kernel. To put it in a nutshell, *nuts* and *nutty* have been part of the language for more than a century, and have always been considered slang. If a person is nuts, nutty as a fruitcake, or off his nut, he's not mentally stable. If we say "he's a tough nut to crack," it's not easy to get him to come around to our way of thinking. And of course, the person who is nuts about something just loves it. If you think this is all an old chestnut, you're calling it a worn-out joke.

The nut even moved into military language during the Battle of the Bulge in World War II. Brigadier General Anthony McAuliffe, known as "Old Crock" to his troops, was asked to surrender Bastogne when his 101st Airborne Division was outnumbered four-to-one. Despite the odds, he reportedly replied, "Nuts!" to the German officer who awaited a reply. There are those who believe that McAuliffe, tough airborne officer that he was, said something much stronger, but no proof has been offered. In any case, *nuts* became an expressive substitute.

Words sometimes do get mixed up. Take the Jordan almond, which comes to us from Spain and has no connection whatsoever to the country Jordan, as many people assume. This delicious nut got its name from the French *jardin almond*, which translates to *garden almond*.

Peanuts take their name from their resemblance to peas in a pod. They are eaten raw, boiled, roasted, salted, or unsalted. *Peanut* is translated into twenty-six languages, with some interesting changes in title. For instance, in Denmark, peanuts are called *little radishes*. The peanut is used in the condescending expression "no comments from the peanut gallery." This referred to the cheapest seats in the house, located in the gallery or second balcony. It was so high up that the spectators sitting there were able to throw peanut shells on performers who displeased them.

Peanut butter was invented in 1890 by an anonymous St. Louis doctor who was looking for a nutritious, digestible food for elderly patients. He ran some peanuts through his meat grinder, added a pinch of salt, and that was the beginning of the peanut butter boom. Even among people with a fondness for the substance, however, there are those who suffer from arachabutyrophobia, a fear of peanut butter on the roof of the mouth.

Nobody has even recorded the identity of the genius who first combined peanut butter with jelly. That famous sandwich is reported to be more American than apple pie. Jelly makes its own statement in the language. We talk about making sure that plans jell together, and we speak of an ineffective person as a jellyfish. Jam, on the other hand, gives us *jam session*, *jammed elevator*, and *traffic jam*. Also, when we're in a predicament, we're in a jam.

From the French *pique*, meaning *to pick*, came *picnic*, a meal taken outdoors and away from home. In America, picnickers usually pack a basket of cold food, sandwiches, and either cans or a thermos of beverage. The outing is usually an upbeat event; hence the expression "it's no picnic" as an understated way to describe something extremely unpleasant.

Available in a variety of forms, noodles are thin strips of pasta. They are prepared as a side dish, in casseroles, or in a delicious noodle pudding. The word itself comes from the German *nudel,* and in 1990, American slang picked it up to describe someone with intelligence and common sense: "That person really uses his noodle."

One of the ingredients that makes the noodle so good is butter, which contributed to some expressions of its own. "To butter someone up" means to flatter him with personal gain in mind. And if a person acts innocent, we might say that "butter wouldn't melt in his mouth."

What is butter without bread? "Half a loaf is better than none" is a common expression today, but it had other shades of meaning when *loaf* appeared from the Old English word *hlaf,* meaning *to rise high.* In spite of this old meaning, the early loaf did not usually rise high; it was either soggy or completely dry because, at that time, leavening was not uniform. Furthermore, it was impossible to get accurate control of oven temperatures.

Enter "the lady." She supervised the work that had to be done around the house. Milking and spinning were done by the girls in the family, but the privilege of making bread—one of the most important items in the diet—was reserved for the housewife herself. She was, therefore, called the *bread kneader* or *lad dige,* an Old English term that later became *lady.*

We think of punch as a beverage usually made of sweetened fruit juices. The theory is that it originally had five ingredients: alcohol, water, lemon, sugar, and spice. According to the legend, the native Indian word *panch*, meaning *five*, was given as the name of this drink.

The world of boxing contributed *punch drunk* to the language. This expression refers to the prize fighter who suffers repeated blows to the head and shows unsteadiness in movement and dull mentality. Describing someone as *punch drunk* has nothing to do with alarming symptoms; it simply means they are befuddled or dazed. It's a temporary feeling that a good night's sleep should cure.

You may have heard the expression "Barmecide's Feast" used to describe an illusion, especially a disappointing one.
According to *The Tales of the Arabian Nights*, Barmecide was a rich, noble prince who belonged to a family of ruling princes in Baghdad. When a poor, starving man named Schacabac came to the prince's castle to beg for food, the nobleman decided to play a cruel practical joke. He invited the beggar to come into the castle and sit at his table to have a feast. Barmecide pretended each plate held a rich delicacy, and Schacabac was forced to praise each imaginary dish for fear he would offend the prince. But the beggar got even. When an empty cup was served, he made believe the wine had gone to his head, and used that as an excuse to hit the prince and knock him to the ground. Barmecide relented. After admitting that he had been wrong to play such a cruel joke, he gave Schacabac a real feast and invited him to share in all the riches of the castle. Barmecide will always be remembered, however, for the imaginary meal he served the beggar.

There's also another type of teasing associated with food. According to Greek mythology, Tantalus, the son of Zeus, pushed his friendship with the gods too far by revealing divine secrets to humans. For his transgression, he was condemned to go forever hungry and thirsty, even though there was always plenty to eat and drink just beyond his reach. His punishment was to stand in water up to his neck while red, juicy grapes and other luscious fruits hung above his head. Each time hunger drove him to reach for the fruit, it was taken away. When we tease someone by keeping something out of reach, we "tantalize."

If you think only food is fried, you'll enjoy this old story from the Texas panhandle.

It tells of a winter so cold that spoken words froze in the air, fell entangled on the ground, and had to be fried in a skillet before the letters would reform to make sense. The idea is an ancient one from the Greek dramatist Aristophanes, who is said to have used it in praising the work of Plato: "As the cold of certain cities is so intense that it freezes the very words we utter, which remain congealed till the heat of the summer thaws them, so the mind of youth is so thoughtless that the wisdom of Plato lies there frozen, as it were, till it is thawed by the refined judgment of age."

One puts food into his mouth, but you've also heard it said: "Every time he opens his mouth, he puts his foot into it." These words were spoken about a Dublin politician, Sir Boyle Roche, whose speeches contained remarks like, "Half the lies our opponent tells about me are not true!"

Perhaps Sir Boyle Roche was also familiar with the expression "to eat one's words," meaning "to have to retract a comment in a humiliating way." There have been many situations when people should have eaten their words, but here is a story that tells of some who actually did. In 1370, the pope sent two delegates with a rolled parchment informing the well-known Bernardo Visconti that he had been excommunicated. Incensed, Visconti arrested the delegates and made them eat the parchment—words, seal, and all.

"To eat crow" is a similar phrase meaning "to be forced into a humiliating situation." The phrase was inspired by an incident that took place during the War of 1812. At that time, it was common for soldiers of both sides to go hunting during an armistice period. One New Englander ventured beyond his boundary and shot a crow when he couldn't find larger game. An unarmed British officer heard the shot, and decided the intruder must be punished. Since he himself had no weapon, the officer complimented the soldier on his shooting and his gun, and then asked to take a look at the weapon. When the naïve New England soldier handed it over, the British officer aimed it at him and ordered him to eat a bite of the crow. The solider was forced to obey. The officer warned him to stay on his own side of the river, and then returned the gun. It was a tactical mistake for the Englishman because the American pointed the gun at him and ordered him to eat the rest of the crow.

The next day, the British officer went to the American commander and explained his side of the story. He demanded that the solider who violated the armistice be punished. The captain had the solider brought in, and asked him whether he had ever before seen the British officer. "Why, yes, Captain," answered the soldier. "I dined with him yesterday."

You Said a Mouthful

//

Eggnog is a rich beverage made with eggs and spirits usually served at Christmastime. The word *nog* is an Old English word for *ale* known in this country since the Revolutionary War.

//

A mericans eat their eggs boiled, hard-boiled, scrambled, poached, shirred, and as an omelet. The egg is the shelled ovum of a bird, especially fowl. The word *egg* comes from the Old Norse word *egg* and is a staple food of the world. Although the eggs of wild fowl, turkeys, geese, ducks, and other birds are eaten, it is the egg of the chicken that is most widely cultivated.

The egg not only gave us special dishes but also broke into the language in a big way.

Describe someone as an egghead and you're talking about someone with a high brow and a receding hairline. The original egghead was Adlai Stevenson, who was bald, intellectual, and a presidential candidate in the United States in 1952.

Eggnog is a rich beverage made with eggs and spirits usually served at Christmastime. The word *nog* is an Old English word for *ale* known in this country since the Revolutionary War.

The eggplant—a deep purple plant related to the potato—is native to India. The name came from its egg-like shape.
The eggplant capitol of the world is Vineland, New Jersey, where half of the commercial eggplants of the eastern part of the United States is

grown and shipped. It has an annual eggplant festival with an eggplant queen dressed in an eggplant-colored gown. The event features a feast of many eggplant dishes topped off with eggplant cake and washed down with eggplant wine.

We talk "egg talk" every day.
The eggshell is worthless once it's cracked and the egg removed, and when we all walk on eggshells, we walk warily. On the old-time farm, where a small flock of hens was a sideline, it was customary for the wife to keep the money from the sale of eggs not required for family use. In those days, this source of funds enabled the housewife to buy clothes, a tablecloth, or anything that caught her fancy.

Put all your eggs in one basket and you've risked everything on a single venture. The expression always makes one think of the fable of the woman who carried all her hopes for the future in her one basket full of eggs, which she dropped while on her way to the market.

In the British game of cricket, a score of zero is called a duck's egg *because of the egg's resemblance to zero.*
Americans picked up the idea for the game of baseball, in which the term was changed to *goose egg*. To fail to score, then, was "to lay an egg on the scoreboard." Today when we fail at anything, it's often described as laying an egg.

If that should happen and you're embarrassed, you might have egg on your face. The beginning of this expression refers to an actor who had rotten eggs thrown in his face for a poor performance.

I don't want to egg you on any further but I'm sure you're aware of the bad egg and the good egg.

It wasn't necessary to dig up Thomas Egg, an American criminal, to account for the bad egg. The strong impression always created by a bad egg is probably why the term came into vogue so much earlier (1853) than the good egg (1914).

The French started the omelet on its career by calling it *alumette*, which was a small metal plate. It also got the additional meaning of eggs beaten and cooked without stirring until set, since such a dish resembled a thin plate. *Alumette* was changed through the years and became *omelet*. "Omelets can't be made without breaking eggs" became a common expression for meaning that some things can't be accomplished without sacrificing others. The phrase is a translation of the French proverb, "*On ne saurait faire une omelet sans casser des oeufs.*"

///

The champagne offered in French
restaurants is a bubbly drink originally
started by Dom Pérignon, a
Benedictine monk from northern
France. He so named the
wine because it was
produced in the Champagne
region of the country.

///

The word *restaurant* is the generally accepted English word used to classify all eateries.

It began as the French *restaurer*, which means *to restore*, and was used to describe a full-fledged public dining room in Paris back in 1765. Over the door was this inscription: "Come to me, all those stomachs that cry out in anguish, and I shall restore you."

The idea of public eating establishments caught on, and today they are called by many different names. Besides the restaurant, there's the cafeteria and the coffee shop, the delicatessen and the bistro, the diner, and even the fast-food stand.

In large cities, restaurants from almost any nationality can be found.
Take, for example, the French restaurant, usually noted for elegant dining. A Cordon Bleu chef is assurance of outstanding cuisine and service, since the term for "blue ribbon" has long been the sign of supremacy.

The champagne offered in French restaurants is a bubbly drink originally started by Dom Pérignon, a Benedictine monk from northern France. He so named the wine because it was produced in the Champagne region of the country.

The word *menu* is also borrowed from France, where it is known as a detailed list. The computer industry picked up the word, and uses it as a list of options from which commands or facilities are selected.

The main course might be a filet mignon, a very tender cut of beef that comes from the French *filet*, meaning *thick slice*, and *mignon*, meaning *dainty*. Salad, which follows the main course in a French restaurant, comes from the Latin word *sal*, meaning *salt*. The reason is that salads originally were topped with little more than simple salt.

The popular Caesar salad has nothing to do with Julius Caesar or any of his relatives. In the late twenties, Caesar Gardini was the owner of a restaurant called Caesar's Place in Tijuana, Mexico. On the July Fourth weekend in 1924, many hungry tourists appeared at his place on their way north to the bullfights. Unprepared for this sudden rush of business, he had to improvise a salad from the food he had on hand. The result was the now-famous Caesar salad.

A parfait made from several different ice creams in the perfect finish to this meal, since *perfect* is exactly what the French *parfait* means.

The bistro started as a small eatery in France.

When Russian troops invaded Paris after the fall of Napoleon in 1815, they raced into restaurants and cafés to eat and drink. They shouted "*Bystro! Bystro!*" ("Quick! Quick!"), which was a command they made in their own restaurants if the service was slow.

Let's change the setting and move on to the delicatessen, which is usually a fancy grocery store that sells cooked meats, prepared foods, and delicacies of ethnic origin.

Each group of immigrants brought its own culinary heritage, which helped to make their strange new world a little more familiar. *Deli-*

catessen comes from the German *delikatessen*, a place where delicate morsels are sold.

Through the years, New York became the nation's delicatessen capital, and today there are many such establishments throughout the country. While most have lengthened their menu, they have also shortened their names to *deli*.

Let's stop at a coffee shop for breakfast.

When we "break the fast" with a bowl of cereal, we pay tribute to Ceres, the goddess of grains, harvest, and agriculture. The ancient Romans believed that only she could answer their prayers for rain. During a terrible drought, they brought sacrifices to the temple they had built for her. When the dry spell ended, they showed their gratitude by naming the grain of the harvest *cerealis*, meaning *of Ceres*.

A different kind of refreshment can be ordered at a saloon, which is a place where alcoholic drinks are sold by the glass, either at the bar or at a table.

The word *saloon* comes from the French *salon*, an elegantly furnished room where fancy Parisian ladies would hold court for distinguished visitors. The word changed by the time it reached the United States. The *salon* became the *saloon* and came to mean a bar or tavern run by a saloon keeper.

Saloon took on an unsavory connotation when Prohibition came along, and even after it was repealed, Americans preferred to use other terms such as *lounge, tavern,* or *inn*.

Some misinformed people think that *booze* is a slang word for liquor, but it really goes back to the German word *bousen*, which means *to drink deeply*.

The word *booze* gained popularity in the United States when a distiller named E. G. Booz had his name stamped on the labels of E. G. Booz's Log Cabin Whiskey. The bottles were blown in the shape of log cabins at the Whitney Glass Works in Philadelphia.

Today, whiskey is still referred to as booze. If you indulge in an occasional "nip," you'll be interested to know that *nip* is simply short for *nipperkin*, a small flask that often holds booze.

One of the most popular items in a Chinese restaurant is chop suey, which did not originate in China, but is genuinely Chinese-American.

Li Hung Chang was the ambassador of China to the United States in 1896. When he came to New York in August of that year, he created a sensation. His entourage included a crew of three cooks, five valets, his personal barber, and thirty-two household servants. He was greeted by President Grover Cleveland, who felt the United States should receive the ambassador in grand style.

The president scheduled a special dinner honoring Chang and informed the White House culinary talent that he wanted an entirely new dish to be served, one that would appeal to both his Chinese and American guests. The result of this request was chop suey. The popularity of the new dish spread across the United States and into China.

Today, chop suey is still prepared as it was on August 29, 1896. If you're skillful, you may eat it with chopsticks, the eating utensils used by the Chinese and Japanese. The name does not refer to chopping food, which would be quite an accomplishment with the two long sticks. It is based on the Chinese word *c'wai*, meaning *quick and nimble*.

Oh, yes, one more little bit of information: The song "Chopsticks" was not named after the Chinese eating utensil. Instead, the title acknowledges that to play this quick little waltz, the hands make a chopping motion.

People look for a fast-food spot when they want to take the small fry for a nosh or a snack.

Nosh means *to nibble* and comes from the German word *naschen*. A snack is food eaten quickly, and it was given to us by the Dutch word *snacken*, meaning *to bite*. And so a snack very properly is a bite to eat.

As for the small fry, the phrase goes back to the Civil War: Harriet Beecher Stowe introduced the expression to describe children in her famous book, *Uncle Tom's Cabin*.

For some Italian flavor, let's eat at a ristorante.

Now, everyone knows that most people do not eat paste, right? Wrong. The Latin word *pasta*, meaning *paste*, is the name for dough. The word passed into Italian, and we borrowed it as the general name for all dough products: spaghetti (little strings), macaroni, vermicelli (little worms), and many more. All are pasta—and the paste that turns into cake is called *pastry*.

A cafeteria is a restaurant where people pick up a tray and move down a line, selecting food and drink displayed along the counter. The word *cafeteria* started off as the name of a Spanish coffee shop, but when Americans adopted it, the term described a self-service restaurant.

Regardless of the type of restaurant, leftovers can be taken home in a doggie bag. Its name suggests that the contents will be fed to the dog, but most people take it for their own enjoyment the next day.

The idea became so popular that some restaurants even have special bags printed with the words "doggie bag." The term now mainly describes leftovers taken home in Styrofoam containers or, from more upscale establishments, wrapped in swans shaped from tin foil.

//

Please take all this food advice with a grain of salt and just beat them to the punch—because you know the apple doesn't fall far from the tree, and you can't get blood out of a turnip.

//

I don't want to put words in your mouth, but when it comes to the universal subject of food, there are many lessons to learn.

We all know that variety is the spice of life, and understand that half a loaf is better than none. And, of course, we're aware that it's a good idea to know which side of your bread is buttered, and how important it is to avoid getting yourself in a pickle—or you'll end up in a kettle of fish.

We also know you can't cry over spilt milk, too many cooks spoil the broth, and it isn't really a good idea to bite off more than you can chew. If you bite the hand that feeds you, you'll be going straight from the frying pan into the fire; your goose will be cooked, and you'll be stewing in your own juice.

Now it's true, sometimes you're a glutton for punishment and you eat your heart out, but try to swallow your pride and eat humble pie.
You know you have to use your noodle and remember that life is just a bowl of cherries. Drink, be merry, and understand that proof of the pudding is in the eating. Of course, after a while things do get to be cut and dried, and you realize there's many a slip 'twixt the cup and the lip.

The glass is half empty and not half full. You do have to watch it or you'll put your foot in your mouth and before you know it, you'll have a red herring on your hands.

We all know you can't take two bites of a cherry, there are other fish to fry, chickens do come home to roost, and before long you'll have them all eating out of your hand.

Please take all this food advice with a grain of salt and just beat them to the punch—because you know the apple doesn't fall far from the tree, and you can't get blood out of a turnip.

It all boils down to this: Don't go on a wild goose chase but handle the situation like a duck in water. Really now, I don't want to take the words out of your mouth, so let's finish this with a glass of champagne and a toast to *You Said a Mouthful*. For you see, every day in every way, we do "eat our words."

BIBLIOGRAPHY

A

Adams, J. Donald. *The Magic and Mystery of Words*. New York: Holt, Rinehart and Winston, 1963.

Ammer, Christine. *Fighting Words*. New York: Laurel Books, 1989.

———. *It's Raining Cats and Dogs*. New York: Dell Publishing, 1989.

Asimov, Isaac. *Books of Facts*. New York: Fawcett Columbine, 1979.

———. *Would You Believe?* New York: Grosset and Dunlap, 1981.

B

Beaudouin, John T. and Everett Mattlin. *The Phrase-droppers Handbook*. Garden City, New York: Doubleday and Company, 1976.

Beeching, Cyril Leslie. *A Dictionary of Eponyms*. Oxford: Oxford University Press, 1988.

Bellafiore, Joseph. *Words at Work*. New York: Amsco School Publications, 1968.

Berlitz, Charles. *Native Tongues*. New York: Grosset and Dunlap, 1982.

Bernardo, Stephanie. *The Ethnic Almanac*. New York: Dolphin Books, 1981.

Bernstein, Theodore. *Miss Thistlebottom's Hobgoblins*. New York: Farrar, Strauss and Giroux, 1971.

Bowler, Peter. *The Superior Person's Book of Words*. Boston: David Gadine, 1982.

Boycott, Rosie. *Batty, Bloomers and Boycott*. New York: Peter Bedrick Books, 1982.

Brandeth, Gyles. *The Joy of Lex*. New York: William Morrow and Company, 1980.

Brasch, R. *How Did It Begin?* New York: David McKay Company, 1967.

Bremner, John B. *Words on Words*. New York: Columbia University Press, 1980.

Brewer, E.C. *Dictionary of Phrase and Fable*. New York: Harper and Row, 1964.

Brock, Suzanne. *Idiom's Delight*. New York: Random House, 1988.

Bromberg, Murray. *Words with a Flair*. New York: Barron's Educational Series, 1979.

Burnham, Tom. *Dictionary of Misinformation*. New York: Thomas Y. Crowell Company, 1975.

C

Campbell, Hannah. *Why Did They Name It...?* New York: Fleet Publishing Corporation, 1964.

Chapman, Bruce. *Why Do We Say Such Things?* New York: Miles-Emmet, 1947.

Ciardi, John. *Browser's Dictionary*. New York: Harper and Row, 1987.

———. *Good Words to You*. New York: Harper and Row, 1987.

Claiborne, Robert. *Loose Cannons and Red Herrings*. New York: Ballantine Books, 1989.

———. *Our Marvelous Native Tongue*. Times Books, 1983.

D

Donaldson, Graham and Sue Setterfield. *Why Do We Say That?* New York: Pennyfarthing Editions, 1986.

E

Ehrlich, Eugene and David H. Scott. *Mene, Mene, Tekel*. New York: Harper Collins, 1990.

Ernst, Margaret. *In a Word*. New York: Harper and Row, 1960.

Espy, Willard. *O Thou Improper, Thou Uncommon Noun.* New York: Clarkson Potter, 1978.

Evans, Bergen. *Comfortable Words.* New York: Random House, 1962.

Evans, Bergen and Cornelia Evans. *Dictionary of Contemporary American Usage.* New York: Random House, 1957.

Ewart, Neil. *Everyday Phrases.* London: Blandford Press, 1983.

F

Feldman, David. *Who Put the Butter in Butterfly?* New York: Harper and Row, 1989.

Ferm, Virgilius. *Brief Dictionary of American Superstitions.* New York: Philosophical Library, 1965.

Flesch, Rudolf. *Lite English.* New York: Crown Publishers, Incorporated, 1983.

Flexner, Stuart Berg. *Dictionary of American Slang.* Pocket Book Edition, 1967.

———. *I Hear America Talking.* New York: Van Nostrand Reinhold Company, 1976.

———. *Listening to America.* New York: Simon and Schuster, 1982.

Funk, Charles Earle. *A Hog on Ice.* New York: Harper and Row, 1948.

Funk, Wilfred. *Word Origins and Their Romantic Stories.* Funk and Wagnall's, 1950.

G

Garraty, John A., ed. *Encyclopedia of American Biography.* New York: Harper and Row, 1974.

Garrison, Webb. *How It Started.* New York: Abingdon Press, 1972.

———. *What's In a Word?* New York: Abingdon Press, 1954.

Gleeson, Paul F. *Rhode Island: The Development of a Democracy.* Providence: Rhode Island State Board of Education, 1957.

H

Hagerman, Paul Stirling, and Myron Miller. *It's a Weird World*. New York: Sterling Publishing, 1990.

Handbook of Commonly Used American Idioms. Barron's Educational Series, Incorporated, 1984.

Harris, Harry. *Yankee Ingenuity*. Chelsea, MI: Scarborough House, 1990.

Hendrickson, Robert. *The Facts On File Encyclopedia of Word and Phrase Origins*. New York: Facts on File, 1987

———. *American Talk*. Harmondsworth, Middlesex, England: Penguin Books Ltd., 1986.

———. *Animal Crackers*. New York: Viking Press, 1983.

Herbruck, Wendell. *Word Histories*. Shakespeare Head Press, 1937.

Heritage Cook Book, Better Homes and Gardens. Meredith Corporation, 1975.

Horowitz, Edward. *Word Detective*. New York: Hart Publishing Company, 1978.

Hunt, Cecil. *Word Origins*. New York: Philosophical Library, 1949.

J

Jacobson, John D. *Toposaurus*. New York: John Wiley and Sons, Incorporated, 1990.

Jennings, Gary. *Personalities of Language*. New York: Thomas Y. Crowell Company, 1965.

———. *World of Words*. New York: Atheneum, 1984.

L

Lass, Abraham H., David Kiremidjian, and Ruth M. Goldstein. *The Facts on File Dictionary of Classical, Biblical & Literary Allusions*. Facts on File, 1987.

Lederer, Richard. *Anguished English*. New York: Dell Publishing, 1987.

———. *Crazy English*. New York: Pocket Books, 1989.

Leokum, Arkady, Paul Posnick, and Stanley J. Corwin. *Where Words Were Born*. Los Angeles: Corwin Books, 1977.

M
Magill, Frank N. *Magill's Quotations*. New York: Harper and Row, 1965.

Manser, Martin. *The Business Book of Words*. Guinness Publishing, Ltd., 1988.

———. *Melba Toast, Bowie's Knife, and Caesar's Wife*. New York: Avon Books, 1988.

Mariani, John F. *The Dictionary of American Food and Drink*. New Haven and New York: Ticknor and Fields, 1983.

Mastfeld, Julius. *Variety Music Cavalcade*. Englewood Cliffs, NJ: Prentice Hall, 1966.

Mathews, Mitford M. *Americanisms*. Chicago: Phoenix Books, 1966.

McDonald, James. *Wordly Wise*. New York: Franklin Watts, 1985.

Mencken, H.L. *The American Language (Two Volumes)*. New York: Alfred A. Knopf, 1966.

Morris, William, ed. *American Heritage Dictionary of the English Language*. Houghton Mifflin Company, 1976.

Morris, William, and Mary Morris. *Dictionary of Word and Phrase Origins*. New York: Harper and Row, 1964.

———. *Dictionary of Word and Phrase Origins*. New York: Harper and Row, 1967.

———. *Harper Dictionary of Contemporary Usage*. New York: Harper and Row, 1975.

McCully, Helen. *Nobody Ever Tells You These Things (About Food and Drink)*. New York: Holt, Rinehart and Winston, 1967.

N
Nurnberg, Maxwell, and Morris Rosenblum. *All About Words*. Englewood, NJ: Prentice Hall, 1966.

O

Orcutt, Georgia, ed. *Yankee Superlatives*. Yankee Press, 1977.

Oxford American Dictionary. New York: Avon Books, 1979.

Oxford Dictionary of Quotations. New York: Oxford University Press, 1979.

Oxford English Dictionary 8th Edition. Oxford: Clarendon Press, 1990.

P

Panati, Charles. *Browser's Book of Beginnings*. Boston: Houghton Mifflin, 1984.

———. *Extraordinary Origins of Everyday Things*. New York: Harper and Row, 1987.

Partridge, Eric. *A Dictionary of Catch Phrases*. Briarcliff Manor, NY: Stein and Day, 1977.

———. *A Dictionary of Clichés*. E.P. Dutton Company, 1963.

———. *Origins, Short Etymological Dictionary*. New York: Crown Publishers, 1983.

Pearl, Anita. *The Jonathan David Dictionary of Popular Slang*. Middle Village, NY: Jonathan David Publishers, Incorporated, 1980.

Q

Quinn, Jim. *American Tongue and Cheek*. Harmondsworth, Middlesex, England: Penguin Books Ltd., 1980.

R

Reader's Digest Association, *Stories Behind Everyday Things*. Pleasantville, NY: 1980.

———. *Success with Words*. Pleasantville, NY: 1983.

Rees, Nigel. *The Phrase that Launched a Thousand Ships*. New York: Dell Publishing, 1991.

Rose, John E., Jr. *Big Words for Big Shooters*. New York: Everest House, 1981.

Rosten, Leo. *Joys of Yiddish*. New York: McGraw Hill Book Company, 1960.

S

Safire, William. *The New Language of Politics*. New York: Random House, 1968.

Sarnoff, Jane and Reynold Ruffins. *Words*. New York: Charles Scribner's Sons, 1981.

Severn, Bill. *Place Words*. New York: Ives Washburn, Incorporated, 1969.

———. *People Words*. New York: Ives Washburn, Incorporated, 1966.

Shipley, Joseph T. *Dictionary of Word Origins*. Totowa, NJ: Littlefield, Adams and Company, 1967.

———. *In Praise of English*. New York: Times Books, 1977.

Smith, Bernie. *Joy of Trivia*. Los Angeles: Brooke House Publishers, 1976.

Smith, Douglas B. *Ever Wonder Why?* New York: Fawcett Gold Medal, 1991.

Sperling, Susan Kelz. *Tenderfeet and Ladyfingers*. Viking Press, 1981.

Stimpson, George. *A Book about a Thousand Things*. New York: Harper and Row, 1946.

T

Train, John. *Remarkable Words*. New York: Clarkson N. Potter, Incorporated, 1980.

Tuleja, Tad. *The Cat's Pajamas*. New York: Fawcett Columbine, 1987.

———. *Curious Customs*. New York: Harmony Books, 1987.

V

Vanoni, Marvin. *I've Got Goose Pimples*. William Morrow Company, 1989.

Varasdi, J. Allen. *Myth Information*. New York: Ballantine Books, 1989.

W

Walk, Allan. *Naming of America*. Nashville and New York: Thomas Nelson, Incorporated, 1977.

Wallechinsky, David, and Irving Wallace. *The People's Almanac*. Doubleday and Company, Incorporated, 1975.

Whitaker, Otto. *Such Language*. Anderson, SC: Droke House, 1969.

About the Author

A native Rhode Islander, Florence Markoff was a pioneer among women broadcasters. She is the writer, producer, and voice of several award-winning radio shows, including "There's a Word for It" and "Rhode Island Portraits in Sound." Her popular shows broadcast for decades to millions of listeners across southern New England. Those listeners continue to acknowledge and recognize Florence by her distinctive radio voice whenever she is out and about. Florence was inducted to the Rhode Island Radio Hall of Fame in 2011, and in 2014 by her alma mater, Emerson College, to the Emerson WERS Hall of Fame. She has also performed one-woman programs before hundreds of audiences throughout her career.

Before becoming a radio celebrity, Florence raised three sons, Joseph, Ron, and Gary, with her husband, Henry, while writing and voicing radio scripts and commercials. *You Said a Mouthful* is an extension of her long-running radio show, "There's a Word for It."

Made in the USA
Middletown, DE
11 June 2017